SAPPHIRE'S SOUL TOOLS

A Beginner's Guide to Spiritual Living

Sapphire Waters

FIRST EDITION
Print Edition

CONTENTS

ACKNOWLEDGMENTS

Thank you to all of my family, my hubby, kids, parents, my sis in law. Thank you to my friends Ashley, Jenni, Brandy, Sensay. My life coach B, and all of the authors who helped with their advice, and knowledge. Thank you to my editor Kendra who spent so many hours coaching and guiding me through this process. Thank you to YOU, for taking the time to read this, for being the change that you wish to see in the world. I love you all!

INTRODUCTION

The Journey begins

Imagine this scene for a moment. You get home from work one day, and your spouse or partner says, "Honey, I have a surprise for you! We are going on a trip."

"A trip!" you say. "Where to?"

"Trust me, you'll love this place."

"Okay, I'll go pack a suitcase."

"Never mind," he says. "We'll just get whatever we need when we get to our destination."

So, you decide to go along with this game. You get in the car, and drive to the airport,; feeling excited for the journey that you're about to embark on. Your spouse doesn't let you see the boarding ticket and hurries you along to the gate and gets you into your seat on the plane.

Before you know it, the pilot announces, "We have landed in ….." As soon as you get off the plane, you realize that you're on an island. You don't have a map, so you don't know how to get anywhere, and the locals don't speak your language.

Some people are brave, and would work this situation to their advantage,; figuring things out along the way. If you're anything like me though, you would probably be freaking out at this point. "What am I going to wear? What am I going to eat? Where will I sleep? What about my makeup?"

That leap into the unknown is exactly what happened to your soul when you decided to make the journey here to Earth. You were given to your parents for specific reasons (without yet knowing why). You agreed to make soul contracts with people. And You came in wanting to learn certain lessons to help you grow. But no one gave you a map or a study guide, to help guide you on your journey. All your soul heard was, "Flight 177 now boarding for Earth!" And your brave soul jumped on for the ride.

Now you're here trying to figure out this life, and the world you're living in, doing the best you can, no doubt., But it can be hard because you weren't given all the information that you needed before you boarded. If, you're like me, you'd be on the phone asking your travel agent what happened to your travel packet.

Life isn't always easy. There are challenges and hardships that we all have to face, even if we don't want to. We all have our personal egos and demons that we must learn how to tame. Sometimes we do it gracefully; at other times we make an ass out of ourselves. The good news, is that you're not alone in this. Every single person who has ever lived in this world has had to make the same journey. Living on Earth is not for the faint of heart or a weak mind. It requires skills that, at one time, I myself thought were impossible.

Here is some more good news. When you find the right tools, such as meditations, affirmations, visualizations, and items such as crystals and oils you will be able to handle more, do more, and be more than you ever thought possible. It's not your fault, or your parents' fault, or anyone else's fault, that you didn't know some of these tools.

When we come to Earth, we're not only taking one journey, we are actually taking two the human and spiritual journeys. The human journey is where we are meant to use our five, sometimes six, senses. Maybe our journey is about understanding our emotions, or at least dealing with them in a constructive way. Maybe it is to repopulate the Earth and to help care for the Earth. Or to have human connections and interactions with others. Our human needs can be easier to fulfill than our spiritual ones. We know that a good diet plan and exercise program can help us stay fit and healthy. That tobacco and too much alcohol are bad for us. These are the things we learned at a fairly young age.

The spiritual journey is intertwined with our physical existence but it is different. The spiritual journey is the soul's journey. If you follow most any kind of religion, then you have no doubt about where your soul goes after you are done here on Earth. But, where did your soul come from in the first place? You are probably well aware of the creation stories – Genesis and the theory of Evolution. What I am talking about is Source. Where your soul originates is one of the most important things for you to know, because it helps you to understand what it came here to learn, why you act the way that you do, and how to deal with the situations that the Earth life will throw at you. This journey to self discovery is going to be messy. You are going to make mistakes, fall down, get up, fall down again .... and by the end of it all, you will have some battle scars to share with others. They will be your stories, your family historys, the proof that you are a warrior in life. And they will be imprinted on your soul. Don't allow the wounds that this world may give you be an excuse to fall into victim mode. See them instead as life's victories.

The purpose of this book is to help you along your path on this journey that we call life. It is my hope that you will be able to use some of the guidance and self-help tools to help light the way for you. You are not alone in this life, even though at times it may feel that way. Spirit is always there to guide you... In this book, I share with you my stories, lessons, challenges, words of wisdom, tools and advice to help you get past the pain and suffering that we all sometimes have.

I know firsthand what happens when the dark side takes over you. For years I felt alone even when I was around other people. I have struggled with anxiety, insecurity, and health problems since I was a teenager – bad hair days, bad weight days, and days where I felt like the world's worst mother. I have yelled at people, cut their throats with my words (sometimes it felt good too!) and have made more mistakes than there are stars in the sky. At times I have played the villain, and at other times, I have played the victim. I have heard that little voice in my head that told me: "This is probably a bad idea, or "You should shut up now," and I have ignored it. I have cried myself to sleep, torn myself apart, and tossed and turned in the middle of the night.

And I discovered that my greatest wish was to help other souls get into the light, so they could be free from suffering, the mindset that they are not good enough, not worthy, not.... To guide them to being the best version of themselves. The world needs you, your gifts, your talents, all your mistakes and failures of the past. Every time you go out into the world as the soul that you are meant to be, you make this planet a better place. Life is nothing but a set of stories perfectly placed chapters all shoved into one incredible book that we call the human experience.

"We are not some casual and meaningless product of evolution each of us is the result of a thought of God, each of us is willed, each of us is loved, each of us is necessary." –Pope Benedict XVI.

The purpose of this book:

This book is a complication of tools, tips and tricks that I have learned along my own journey. It is meant to be used resource to find what works for you. I hope it will inspire you to grow and live the life that your soul came here to live. Through these pages you will learn about your soul, the ego, emotions, beliefs, guides, angel numbers and so much more! All of which are to help you on your journey. As you will soon find out, some of the topics come up in different areas. I have allowed this because like all things it is all connected.

How to Use This Book:

You are really going to want to have some notebook they have mini ones that come in a three pack for around one dollar. I would like you to get a full size notebook as you will use it alongside the rest of this book and hopefully keep using it after. This next one will be your home book. While the mini notebook is meant to be carried with you in your purse or on you in some way so that way when you need the extra strength and support in the heat of any moments, you can stop and take out your book. It's about you. You are the author, the illustrator, and the main character in all of those books. They will guide you on the rest of your journey while here on Earth. I would like you to also have paper and index cards on hand because you will need them to write your affirmations on.

Any quote, mantra, or affirmations that you see, or hear that resonate with your soul I would like you to write down. You can in either your mini notebook, or you can write them on your index cards, or sticky notes. Some of them I will suggest writing down, but really just go with your own gut.

You can also use a tablet, or phone and have notes, quotes and affirmations kept right on your devices.

Head phones would also be wise to have on hand, because during this journey you will be asked to start listening to guided meditations.

PART ONE

Understanding who we are

CHAPTER 1

Is it the Soul or the Ego that is the question

It is said that your body runs like a machine, and your brain is the computer that controls everything. Science has told you about the different wires that you have connecting to different parts of your body. The Soul would be your hard drive, storing all the different "standard" characteristics that you have as a human. The ego would be your software that needs frequent updates. Let me explain to you my beliefs on the soul and the ego.

The Soul

The soul is the spiritual part of a person or animal or even a plant. It is infinite, immortal, and has no end. You can't see your soul but it doesn't make it any less real. You can't, see gravity either but science has proven its existence. The soul is talked about in many religions. Catholics believe that the soul will eventually go up to heaven if the person has lived a selfless and giving life, Muslims believe that the soul comes into existence the moment that the body does. Buddhists say that the soul will keep reincarnated until it has learned all of the lessons that it needed to. In Hinduism, the soul is thought of as being eternal but is trapped in a human body. **The soul came** here to learn and grow. Earth is a good place to learn at a rapid speed.

The Ego

Our next word is EGO and like any of these words there are multiple ways of describing this but here is what Collinsdictionary.com says:

"Someone's ego is their sense of their self-worth."

1. The self of a person; the conscious subject
2. psychoanalysis
The conscious mind, based on the perception of the environment from birth onwards: responsible for modifying the antisocial instincts of the id and itself modified by the conscience (superego)
3. One's image of oneself

Urbandictionary.com says this: "Ego, the part that defines itself as a personality, separates itself from the outside world, and considers itself (read: you) a separate entity from the rest of nature and the cosmos. Perhaps necessary for the survival in some evolutionary bygone, in modern times it leads only to (albeit often disguised) misanthropic beliefs and delusion.

In short, "I". Ego is responsible for hate, fear, and, delusion.

In Christianity ego is said to have seven heads. It is said it is the seven demons that Christ expelled from Mary Magdalene and they are: Lust, Pride, Envy, Wrath, Greed, Gluttony and, Sloth.

Most of the thoughts that we have come from this part and this is what the ego is.

It can show up in many forms for each of us and it follows right along the path of suffering. When our neighbor has the new car that we want and we are trapped in jealousy (ego)

When our spouse makes us angry and we lash out at them yelling things we have rage (ego).

Some may ask why these are also considered sins and the reason why is because these things diminish the amount and quality of the love and compassion that you have towards others. These qualities since they have to do with the ego are self-serving and selfish where others get hurt. I have noticed that when one person verbally attacks another person, that is hidden in that anger the ego is lurking.

For anyone who has ever read *The Power of Now* by Eckert Tolle, you have learned the difference between the soul and the ego. Your soul cares for others – not just your "self." The soul wouldn't hurt another person because your soul knows that you would just be hurting yourself. The reason is that we are all connected. The soul is the source of your inspiration. It gives you your creative ideas, the gifts, and talents that each one of us has. But the ego doesn't understand this, the ego only thinks of what will help it keep its' power.

The ego (unlike the soul) cares only for itself. It will say anything to you so that it doesn't lose its power on the throne. It wants to be in charge of everything that you are doing, saying, and feeling. Its attitude is: 'I should be allowed to do what I want, when I want, and not have to answer to anyone.' It is the thoughts that tell you: 'I'm not good enough,' or 'I want it my way and I don't care about how it affects anyone other than me.' The soul considers others and what benefits all, whereas the ego thinks of what will benefit the ego.

The ego can be a cruel bastard, a snake waiting to strike at the very moment when you're at your weakest point. I have gone through different stages in how I have felt about my ego. At first, I thought it was a voice in my head that I couldn't control. This turned out to be a myth. We can control the thoughts in our heads. In the next stage, I thought the ego was the voice that I had to listen to before I did anything, my little *Judge Judy* giving me input on how I did everything: my hair, my nails, makeup, mothering. You name it and that little Judge Judy was sure to be there giving me a piece of her mind. "Your hair is too frizzy, go redo it." "Your eyeliner is uneven, go fix it." You don't have to listen to *Judge Judy* either.

Then there is the ego as a *tiny child* – you probably know what I am talking about. This is where you see a therapist who explains to you that there is a little girl in a cage and you need to go into your mind, let her out, and comfort her. Shamans also do this kind of work, but it's called soul retrieval and releases past lives.

The *Diva* ego is my name for the one who wants things done their way and there is no room for compromise. It's where you say things you shouldn't and give yourself justification through entitlement. Sometimes it helps to go back to your inner child, but instead of her being in a cage, you'll find her on the floor having a fit.

At times I get mad at my ego, and say to it: "Shut up," or "You're wrong, You're right" – or just straight up, "Go away." I don't recommend this though, it only made things more difficult. The ego will never go away, it will never be reasoned with and negativity towards it will never work. The ego does have one positive quality, and that is to show us what we need to fix, change, or heal inside of ourselves. If you experience a painful memory, instead of falling into a state of negativity, you can say *"Thank you."*

Eckert Tolle has an exercise in *The Power of Now* that you can use to help you see the difference between the soul and the ego. I have a similar one that I would like you to try.

Close your eyes for a moment and imagine there is a big T.V. screen in front of you. On that screen, I want you to watch the thoughts that are being visually displayed. These thoughts may come in the form of words or pictures. There is no wrong way to do this. For example, you may be tthinkin, 'I have to get the house clean today because I have guests coming over tomorrow. Their house is always so clean. If I don't have everything clean enough, they will judge me and tell other people how messy my house was.'

Those thoughts are from your ego. But what or who is watching those thoughts flashing across the T.V. screen? If your ego is busy displaying the thoughts, then surely it can't be the one watching it too, right? The answer is that your soul is the one watching the thoughts. It is also known as the "witness" or the "presence" that is watching this all happen.

How you feel is largely based on what you are thinking. The thoughts that you're having are creating stories. So, when you are watching this screen in the mind, what is the story that you are telling yourself? If your house isn't clean enough, does that mean you aren't good enough? Whether your house is clean enough makes no difference on who you are as a person. It simply means that your house isn't as clean as you would like. For contrast, watch the T.V. show "Hoarders." To those people, your house would look spotless. We all see differently. We all have different stories that we tell ourselves. If you don't like the story that is airing on your T.V., then change the channel. Remember, YOU are the one who is holding the remote.

Part of coming to Earth means that we were given different roles to play. Wife, mother, daughter, aunt, friend, teacher, healer, traveler – these are the common "roles" in my life. But those roles aren't who I am in my soul, and your roles aren't you in your soul. They are our human roles. How I "act" as a wife towards my husband is very different from how I act towards a friend. When we die, those roles die too, because they served us as humans but were not our soul. Your soul is infinite, it will never end. Whether you believe in Heaven and Hell or reincarnation this fact holds true. Either your soul will go to a final resting place or it will come back. Whichever you believe, it doesn't matter. What matters is that you know that your soul has a job to do while it is here on Earth. Your job as a human is to move your ego aside and let your soul do the job that it was meant to do here. I know that sounds easier said than done. But it's true. The faster you learn to allow your soul to be the driver (instead of the ego), the faster you will get out of the pain and suffering.

Everyone has moments in life where they have felt their soul. Some of you may have felt your soul when you became a mom or dad and held your baby for the first time. Or maybe you felt it when you accomplished a goal you'd been working on for a long time. It could be the feeling you had when you saw that old lady struggling with her groceries, and you took the time to load them in the car for her, treating her as if she were your own grandmother. Or maybe you saw a child at school that you knew was having a hard day and you gave them a warm hug or an encouraging word. The soul gives you a feeling inside that the ego can't. The feeling that tugs at your heart strings. It's a mixture of peace, joy, and compassion. I call it the human connection.

When it comes to the soul, no matter what you believe, we all know that there is something more to our existence here on Earth. Our human body will grow old; it will fall apart and fade away – just like the leaves that change through the seasons. In spring the trees are bright and beautiful with blossoms; in summer the foliage will be green and bright; in the fall as the weather turns cooler, the leaves turn magnificent colors of red, orange, and yellow. Finally in winter, the leaves wither and die to become a part of the ground again in the cycle of life. But when we see the winter tree we don't know if the tree is alive or dead, because it looks brown and bare. Only in the spring will we find out whether the tree survived. Our body will do the same, but the soul will go on – whether it's to heaven, or another dimension, or another life is really anyone's guess. But we know that we aren't meant to be here on Earth forever.

Stephanie Meyer gives a perfect example of how I like to visualize the soul in *The Host*. In the movie version of her book, the soul shines as a beautiful silver light at the base of the neck. Souls living in this place all trust each other. They don't lock their cars, or houses, or anything like that. The soul is pure, and helps other souls without asking questions. But then there are ones who are part of the resistance, like the lead character Melanie. She hears this little voice in her head that keeps telling her, "You'll never get rid of me. This is my body." The soul is saying, 'Can't we just get along and go through this together?' But our voice or ego says: 'There is no way I will ever let you be in charge of this body.' Sure, you can let the ego keep being the one in charge, but then you will have more pain and suffering for it. You are always going to experience fear and worry. But what you will learn here is how to not let the fears and worries stop you from being who you really are – in your soul.

Quotes about the Ego:

1. "You can either be a host to God or a hostage to your ego. It's your call." Wayne Dryer
2. "When the ego dies, the soul awakens" Mahatma Gandhi
3. "Complaining is one of the ego's favorite strategies for strengthening itself.' Eckhart Tolle
4. "When ego is lost, limit is lost. You become infinite, kind, beautiful." Harbhajan Singh Yogi
5. "Your ego is your self-image created by thought. It's your social mask requiring validation in fear of losing its sense of identity. "Thibaut
6. "Mastering others is strength. Mastering yourself is true power." Lao Tzu
7. "If someone corrects you, and you feel offended, then you have a problem with the ego." Matthew McConaughey

Affirmations for Ego:

1. It is easy for me to set my ego aside.
2. I love and accept myself.
3. I allow my soul to lead the way, as my ego diminishes more and more.

When the ego talks, listen for a minute to hear what it has to say. Then thank it for giving you its opinion on the matter and move to the next thought. It's important to learn by listening. But the way the ego communicates with us is not only through our thoughts. It is through our emotions.

CHAPTER 2

Getting in Touch with our Emotions and Getting to Know (and Overcome) our Beliefs

In the last chapter I talked about how the ego can give you your thoughts. Here you will see how those thoughts create our emotions. If you have a negative thought, then you will also have a negative feeling. Life teaches us the definitions of things. We can read what the dictionary, or google has said they are, but the truth is we learn by feelings. Here is my definition of a feeling:

Feelings

This word has two meanings that are very important to understand.

1. An emotional state or a reaction. When the emotion hits you, you are having a reaction to something that is going on.

2. A belief especially an IRRATIONAL one (negative, not your truth kind of belief). Read this again when you are having a feeling come up you are having a belief that you have come up. So if the feeling is coming up in the form of fear, you are being shown that you have a belief in there that is causing you to feel fearful. For example let's say in the past your car got broken into when you were a teenager. Five years later you still may get into a panic if you locked your car because in the past

your car was broken into. So the belief there is "My car is going to get broken into all the time." you forgot how many more times your car DIDN'T get broken into.

One of my clients has a fabulous view point on this that I have to admire.

One day my client/friend and I were going to get me my pink hair dye at the local beauty supply store. She drove us there and we joked about it being in the ghetto part of town. We hopped out of the vehicle and she just left her windows down and the car unlocked.

Aren't you going to lock it? I asked.

"No!" She said.

Why? I asked.

"Because I use to live in Seattle and I learned that it doesn't matter if you lock it or not if someone wants to steal something they will find a way, I have replaced to many windows for a few dollars and a stupid phone cord. They can have it!"

What a wonderful belief she has. She doesn't feel fear every time she leaves her car in a parking lot. She simply accepts that it may or may not happen and that she is ok even if it does. She feels safe in the world and her actions show this. That's why everyone tries to tell us that if we change our beliefs then we change our lives.

There's a game that I play with my children to help them with the situation or circumstance is "the car" and the emotion they are having at the time, such as anger, fear…. is "the driver." It teaches them about their emotions, and how to identify a negative emotion and change it for a positive one.

For example, when my son gets upset because he asked his sister to play with him and she says no, he will instantly start picking on her. So I say to him, "Why are you acting this way?"

His response: "Because I am angry."

From there, I make him consider this: "You are the one who is driving the car. Who are you letting drive?"

"Anger," he will say.

"Who do you want to be driving the car?"

"Joy," he says.

"Then change the driver."

An actual emotion lasts only ninety seconds. After that, only thoughts run through the mind. But those thoughts will drive your actions, as in the case of my son or my daughter (she does it to him too). He got angry because his sister wouldn't play with him. So the thoughts that came were anger driven, resulting in annoying her until she cried. Change your thoughts to positive one, and you'll change your actions to the positive too. You have a choice in how to respond.

Happiness is a choice no matter what anyone says. Yes, you will always go through stuff in life that pushes your buttons, but you always have the choice to say: "Even though [fill in the blank] is happening, I still choose to find the good in it. Even if I can't see it right now."

Getting in touch with your Feelings:

The emotions are the first thing that you need to have an understanding of while doing this soul journey. Emotions aren't "bad." Trust me on that. Coming from a very sensitive person, for me to say that, says a lot. Your emotions are trying to tell you something.

All anger stems from hurt. If you are angry with someone, it is because something inside of you is hurting. In Michael Alan Singer's book, *The Untethered Soul*, he explains that when your chest tightens, that energy needs to be released. That energy comes up because something inside of us has been triggered. And it wasn't necessarily because of something going on at that moment. It could be caused by something that happened years ago in childhood, where most of our fears and worries originate. You don't even have to remember the event for it to trigger you. When it comes up though, it's important for you to *release it*. When strong feelings come up, you are offered two choices to make it through those ninety seconds. You can either feel it, even though it hurts, or you can say, "No, I am not dealing with this. I am just going to shove it down and ignore it." The second choice may give you some temporary relief, but I assure you that the pain will come back up at some point.

As my life coach, Bernadette Logue, would say, the emotional pain will show up in a "different costume." You may not even know why you feel bad, you will just know that you are being triggered and it's hurting.

Hidden Layers:

Most of us are familiar with anger, but in most situations you have to dig deeper, go below the layer of anger and find out what other layers are hidden beneath the surface. The ones that I find (so far) in other souls, including myself are:

Suffering

The state of undergoing pain, distress and hardship.

That is what google says about suffering.

I consider suffering the stomach pain that I have when I am thinking too much about tomorrow when I am supposed to be going to sleep. The questions that I have that say "Are you really enough?", "What are you going to do about ..."

I also link this one to the ego. The ego is the one that causes our suffering. It uses our thoughts against us in that way. The ego isn't evil or anything. It was just taught by the beliefs that we have and when those beliefs aren't kind we cause ourselves suffering. If you change the way that you see a situation you can eliminate the suffering, the pain and you begin to turn your ego into your friend. Instead of it telling you that you can't it will tell you that you can.

Grief

You feel grief when something really sad happens in your life. Grief means an "Intense sorrow." Some say that there are different stages of grief that when we go through things like the death of a loved one or a divorce we will go through. They are shock and denial, pain and guilt, anger and bargaining, depression, reflection and loneliness, the upward turn, recon-struction and working through, and acceptance and hope. It is possible to go through these stages very quickly, being through them all in a matter of weeks or you can spend months or even years stuck in each one. One of my clients was the first one to tell me about these stages of grief. She had told me how long she was going to grieve and then she would let it go. Her time frame was very long and I asked her" Why do you have a deadline that you are trying to make it to?" Why does it have to be that long? The only thing that she could tell me is that "I don't know I just read it in a book." Now because she is also my friend I was able to go about things a little differently with her than I would someone else. I am not heartless. I have lost many things. Loved ones, friends, animals and I are super sensitive so these all have affected me on a deep level but instead of staying stuck in them I move faster through.

The Buddhist belief is very different from ours. They understand the concept of impermanence. That life is a cycle of death and rebirth. They see death as just a transition from this life to the next. Divorce can be seen in the same way. "When one door closes another one opens". I have heard that some celebrate death for the person that passed on because now that person is no longer in suffering. In Christianity, we say "Well now they are up in heaven with Jesus and free from pain". So I can understand where they are all coming from in this.

When my daughter's bunny died in the Spring of 2020 I asked her to tell me what grieving is for her. She explained that for her, it was a feeling. It was a pain in her chest and she just wanted to cry. We *Peaced* (breathing in peace) and *Released* the pain in her chest and I told her to cry, it's a form of release. Then we tried a Buddhist / spiritual way to handle this. She had prayed to God to take her bunny's soul up to heaven, then we laughed as we shifted the thoughts of suffering and sadness into remembrance through laughter, and we ended it with doing a meditation where her heart chakra connected up into the energy of her bunny. I taught her that instead of thinking of her bunny and being sad, to think of her and send her love whenever she does. If you start to think of someone that you have lost in anyway instead of being sad stop yourself. It's ok to say I miss …. Because you have to accept your feelings but then instead of staying stuck in the sadness say *I miss (person, animal, thing) and I am choosing to send them some love and light.*

Hate

Hate is an emotion, an intense form of anger. It invokes feelings such as resentment. The reason why it is there is because of the pent up anger that we don't let go of. Some call it bottling up making it sound like a soda. Well if that is the case then hate is what happens when you shake the soda. It explodes and makes a huge mess wherever it is. Nothing good ever comes from hate. If you dig deeper to why you have hate and anger in the first place you would most likely see that it is from something such as not feeling heard, not feeling appreciated, and not accepting something about a situation. The feelings you caused yourself by your beliefs (I am" not heard" is very different than my loved one didn't hear me.) Not accepting something is of course going to throw you into feelings of anger and hate but again you are causing your own feelings.

If your stomach hurts for more than three days then your body is telling you that you are hanging onto anger. Listen to your body, forgive and move on.

Ask yourself *What do I have to gain by hanging on to this anger? What do I have to lose by letting this anger go?*

Jealousy

Jealousy is another negative feeling that we humans tend to get. It comes because we do not have enough trust in ourselves and usually pops up in the form of anger. Some call it the green eyed monster. Jealousy is a hard human emotion; it is the breeding ground for violence of the mind and violence towards others. It makes us feel insecure about who we are and what our place is in the world.

Envy is wanting what someone else has where jealousy is a fear, a belief that you have that something you care about will be taken from you by someone else. Jealousy can come in many forms and the severity differs from person to person and situation to situation. Again though when you dig deep into it you will find that the Jealousy is brought on by the beliefs that you have. If you are insecure then you must change the beliefs to be secure and confident in order to be free from jealousy.

Breathe and Release

So, what do you do when this energy comes up? The solution is simple – yet hard to do. You let it go by breathing. You breathe your way through it. I like to breathe in peace and then release. That is also what I say "I breathe in peace, and now I release." until the tightening lets go. When I focus on my breathing, I don't give my ego (my self-critic) time to come in and give me its two cents. I don't need to know its opinion on the matter. I just need to focus on the fact that if I truly want this uncomfortable pain to go away, I must face it head on. Facing it doesn't mean trying to rationalize it. It just means remembering to catch myself before I allow the thoughts to come in, and breathing through it all. At first it is hard. But it will get easier with time, as you develop a new habit of how to deal with your negative emotions. Breathe… and release.

I know some people who like to dive into the pain or discomfort and ask, "Why am I feeling this way?" And then they get an answer: "Because they embarrassed me," or "Because they abandoned me and now I feel alone." This is another good way to handle the emotions. This process gives you clarity, which helps you to release even more. Release is the key here.

You either release the emotion or you grow it. I like to say to myself, 'I don't know why I am feeling this way and I don't need to know why. I just need to release it.' I tell myself, 'If I can make it through these ninety seconds, I won't cause myself anymore damage.' This method has worked well for me, though it may not work for you. Experiment to see what works best.

Yoga

Yoga is another good way to get the mind, body, and soul on board with this Earth Journey. I am not a fan of strenuous exercise. Yoga is gentle enough that we can do it more easily than aerobic exercise, and it gets everything working together at once – the person functions as a whole. Now I don't know about you, but I would rather hit two birds with one stone, and this approach is more like hitting three birds. If you have physical pain, let's say, in your back, it will also help with that. Coming from experience, it works wonders. There are many different kinds of yoga, so you can shop around and see what works for you. Take a few workshops or try some online video classes.

In *Midnights with a Mystic*, Indian yogi and author Sadhguru Jaggi Vasudev says, "Once you are a yogi, nothing bad can ever happen to you again because there is nothing that you cannot use for your ultimate growth. Even in hell a yogi can be happy. If you are happy there is no such thing as hell."

The moment I read that quote, I immediately texted it to Sensay, my Reiki master and friend. I call her "Sensay" because she is so enlightened (Sensei is the Japanese word for master teacher). She is also a yoga teacher; spirituality is at the forefront of all her actions. For weeks, I had been picking her brain on how she handles things. I had been on this spiritual journey for years, too, getting good tips, advice, and actions (such as reiki healing, coaching etc. ...) from all kinds of spiritual people. But Sensay bugged me puzzled me. We would sit together talking about different situations that we'd been through. I could feel my chest tighten as I talked about certain experiences, but hers didn't seem to faze her at all. It seemed as if everything came more easily for her. In truth, she pissed me off because she made it all look so easy. When I sent her that quote, she told me that I had finally figured out the secret to how she dealt with life. She agreed with it 100%. Since then, I have been taking a yoga class once a week when I don't get called in to sub or have a kid home with me. I love how my instructor guides us. She has us take a moment in the beginning to breath and be there now she usually has us do a mediation over one of the elements (air, fire, water, earth) and then we move on to doing the yoga poses, the end is my favorite part though. When we have finished our last pose, she has us lay down on our yoga mats. She comes around and puts a blanket on us and tucks us in if we need it.

After she goes and sits down and uses the singing bowl to gently have us get into a relaxed state of mind. Calming our breathing, she may give us something that she wants us to think about as we drift into this other state of mind. Sometimes she just lets us lay in the peace of the silence. It is so tranquil and zen that a part of me is always bummed when I hear the sweet sound of the singing bowl pulling me back into the reality of the Earth world.

I haven't been to any other yoga class so I don't know if it is something that is done everywhere like this but if it is I am totally in and I would recommend that to you too!

I have felt the benefits of yoga first hand.

When it comes to dealing with the ego, I think part of the trick is learning how to communicate with it. The ego is never going to go away. You will have it until the day that you die. However, once you make it your friend, you can learn to partner with it instead of battling with it.

I'm not saying that this is the friend you call up when you have a problem with your man, or this is the one you invite to go shopping with you at the mall. No, this is not that kind of friend. This is the "friend" that calls on you – when you're busy, when you're having a bad day, when your life seems to be at rock bottom, and all the ego wants to do is complain. As we go through life, most of us just let this friend complain. Sometimes we offer our advice, but this "friend" doesn't want to hear the advice, and then we go on with our day. We may listen to their opinion, but we don't have to change who we are for them. Yoga helps slow down the mind, connects the body, and frees the soul.

So now we know that the ego talks to us through our emotions, but where do some of thoughts that feed our emotions come from?

Beliefs

What you believe about yourself, your life, and the world all have a direct impact on your emotions. Anyone who knows about the law of attraction knows this truth. What you believe turns into what you feel, and that feeling vibration turns into what you attract in your life – both the good and the bad. So, in order to change the emotions and thoughts, we must work on changing what we believe.

Albert Einstein said, *"The most important decision we make is whether we believe in a friendly or hostile universe."* Why do you think that is? It's because if you think that you live in a friendly universe, then your interactions with the other people on this planet are generally going to be more positive. But if you think that you live in a hostile universe, where everyone is rude and out for themselves, then that is what you are going to get in return, because that is what you are attracting.

I have seen the definition of belief on both Google and Pinterest. Google has it as a noun where Pinterest has it as a verb. Both of them have similar definitions but here is mine:

> *Belief* – The knowing that something is true, even without proof. It's having trust, and confidence in someone or something. It's believing without seeing. When you have so much faith in something, that even if the whole world is against you on it, you don't compromise it.

In Rhonda Byrne's film, *The Secret*, Rhonda goes on a search talking with amazing people from all walks of life and in different situations about the secret of their success. And they all tell the same story. It's the law of attraction. They give you ways that you can use this law to your advantage. All of them told stories about rough times that they had to overcame. One had cancer, one was paralyzed, another was heart broken. And all of them changed their lives in a positive way the moment they learned to use "The Secret."

At first, when I heard them talk about how easy it was to attract money and abundance into your life, I laughed. They talked about bills that come in the mail. And how to make them disappear. At the time, I was calling bills my "hate mail." There were so many. After watching *The Secret* though, I said jokingly that I was going to call the mailbox, "The Magic Money Box." I had started it as a joke, only believing half of what they had said about the "secret."

About five days later, I walked up to The Magic Money Box and didn't have any bills! Instead I found ten dollars cash. I received a survey with instructions saying that if I did it, they would send me more money. It worked! This kept happening, I kept receiving more surveys. Now the surveys take me one minute to do, so it's really effortless.

Whereas before I would say, 'I am broke.' Now I started telling myself, 'I am a money magnet'.

One day during winter break right before Christmas, I bribed my kids. I told them that if they cleaned the house with me, whatever money we found in the different rooms could be used to buy snacks and sodas for family time over the weekend.

As I was sweeping the living room and getting ready to vacuum the couch, which is the equivalent of a Dumbo size piggy bank, I repeated out loud, "I am a money magnet... I am a money magnet... I am a money magnet."

My daughter stopped and watched me with a confused look on her face and finally asked, "Mom, why are you saying that?"

Because, if the universe is like Aladdin and his lamp, I said, "all I have to do is ask, believe, and receive. When I say I am a money magnet, then I am open and ready to receive."

She nodded her head and started saying it as well. Pretty soon she found a dollar and got very excited because it had worked; so now she had a feeling for it. A few minutes later I found a scratch ticket in the couch that we won five dollars on. So now I was feeling it more and was more excited. My son looked at both of us and then we heard him say, "I am a money magnet!" We ended up cleaning only three rooms in our house that day, from top to bottom, but we had gathered over seventeen dollars. It was amazing!

As it turned out, we didn't buy snacks with that money. My soul spoke up that day instead. So, I talked with my children and told them I would still buy them a special snack, but I wanted to take that money and give a child a special Christmas. Not only did the kids agree, but for the whole next week they cleaned the house and found more money to add to it. We had about thirty dollars by the time we went to Walmart to buy some gifts for the child that we picked off the giving tree at the school. We were able to buy her everything that she had asked for, and we felt good for being able to.

People and their beliefs fascinate me – money beliefs, especially, because they are so powerful. It frustrates many people in my life, but whenever I see someone on the street corner holding a sign asking for money, I give it to them. I always over-tip the waitresses (I was one once myself, so I really get this one). I donate to charities and we give generously to our church.

People lecture me on how some of the homeless people on the street are scammers. They have even seen it with their own eyes. One of them watched a homeless person standing there with a sign, and then at the end of the day, he went and got into his BMW. Even my daughter said to me one day, "Mom, why do you do that when they are just going to spend it on alcohol or drugs? Everyone has already told you how they have seen those same people do things with that money."

Now, I am not denying that some people are scammers. I am not naïve. But here is my belief on this. How people treat you is their karma, how you react is yours. So, using this belief, if I have the money, then I hope that they need it more than me. If they scammed me, then that is on them. Even if twenty out of twenty-one of them were scammers, then at least that one person got the help they needed. If I were that person, I sure hope that someone would come along and help me. I don't ask questions. I just see that they need help and try to help. Sometimes I'll buy them food and write an inspiring quote for them on the receipt. I don't know their story, nor do I need to. All I know is they asked for help and I could give it. *See a need, fill a need* is a motto in our house.

Look at it from the other end. Have you ever asked for help? How did you feel when someone helped you out? Now think of a time when you asked for help and someone said no! How did you feel then? Whenever you come into contact with people, you either lift them up or you bring them down. Which would you rather do? If you believe people are cheaters, liars and thieves, then you're more likely to be miserable and do things that hurt yourself and others.

There is a difference between good people who make bad choices (because we are all human and make mistakes that you later regret), and bad people who intentionally make bad choices that hurt others. We must believe that people are generally good. If we don't, then we will create a life that is based largely on fear. Most likely, the fear of getting hurt. Even with positive beliefs, you still are going to run into pain and fear; the difference is that you won't stay stuck there. You remember that, just like you, everyone makes mistakes, and no one is perfect. We all do things in our own way, according to our own beliefs, and in our own time. When it happens that something triggers us, we are faced with the choice – to keep the pain alive or allow the pain from the situation to pass.

Religious beliefs can help push you forward

Do you know why people who actively follow their faith and go to church regularly seem happier? It's because of their beliefs. You have to have beliefs as a human while you are here on Earth. If you don't know what you believe in, then you will believe in anything until your beliefs are strong enough to be unshaken.

Believing what it says in the bible is not a bad thing, in my view. I think it's all religions have some aspects are similar and whether you believe in God/Universe / Source that it is all the same, just different names. The ten commandments are common sense. Don't steal, don't murder (which is different than kill), don't cheat, etc. The one I struggled with was "Love thy neighbor as thyself." I was more of an old testament "eye for an eye" person. Most of us when we get mad at someone have gone that way before. That dead end route of revenge. But when you start to really believe in loving others in that uncon-ditional way, then you change how you treat others.

Another belief that religion has, is that even if they physical-ly don't have someone there holding them, they still are unconditionally loved and forgiven; no matter what they have done. They might doubt it sometimes as we all do, but the belief is strong enough that you are always pulled back into the truth. So whether you believe in God or a higher power, know you are loved and forgiven. All you have to do is ask.

If you don't think you believe in anything, then find out what you do believe in. There will always be a void that will be filled with a negative until you do so. Some of you may be ready to hear the things that I am telling you as you journey through this book. Some of you will understand fully, while for others, it will open the door to possibility and it will encourage you to dig deeper and find what works for you. I encourage you to go through it. Go through the fears, pain, and heartache. If you are so unhappy, then you couldn't possibly be any unhappier than you already are. There's nowhere to go but up from here, as the saying goes. Take what resonates and just leave the rest.

Picking up Beliefs:

Sometimes the beliefs that we pick up are not our own, they are beliefs that we were exposed to. There are many ways that we can pick up beliefs. The news, magazines, ads, even the people who are apart of our daily life.

Something I want to stress about this human journey is that you have thoughts going on in your head all the time. In our heads we have a narrator that is giving meaning to everything that you do. It is a version of a story. When you tell a story over and over again to yourself, you memorize it. It then becomes a belief. Some people pick up beliefs due to someone else's emotional state. All through school I struggled with learning. I was always in the intervention classes and afterschool pro-grams that give you extra academic support. When I was in 7th grade we had a substitute math teacher one day. I hated math, I didn't understand it, I didn't like it and I was sick of spending hours a day on it. So I am sure that the energy I was producing wasn't of a positive nature. I was trying to understand the lesson she was showing us on the board, but I was behind and felt she was moving too fast. I raised my hand and asked her to come help me because I didn't "get it." She came over and explained what she had written, and I asked her to go back and explain some of the other steps. She did, but I still couldn't grasp it. I was frustrated and was feeling stupid that all my classmates were able to do their work just fine and I couldn't.

"I still don't get it," I snapped.

"You don't get it because you're stupid," she said.

This wasn't the first time I had heard this. My brother called me stupid when he would get angry, and my grandmother had called me that once. Even some of the other kids had, both playfully and in seriousness, and since I was already thinking that myself, I allowed it to be my confirmation. The story I had been telling myself that "I am stupid" was just proven to be true. I now had more proof. I of course responded by slamming my book shut, shoving it off my desk (might have gone across the room, the details are a little fuzzy) and saying something on the lines of, "At least I'm not a fat cow." I then walked out of the classroom and down to the office. I struggled the rest of the year and into the next with math.

They put me in more "special" classes where I barely even tried because I figured, what was the point? However, my "special" math class is where I disproved this belief. I had a kind teacher whose name was Mrs. G, and she sat down to work with me. I thought she was going to be like the other teacher, so I sat there silent and frustrated. Mrs. G sat there with me, day after day, going over all the old lessons. Then one day, she found the lesson that I needed so I could understand the harder ones. It was as if something in my brain had suddenly clicked and it all came together. Mrs. G celebrated with me, giving me a high five and telling me that she knew I could do it. The story she told about me was not that I was just some stupid girl, but the story that "Here is a girl who needs kindness, patience, and understanding, and I am a person who can give that to her." Thanks Mrs. G – your kindness was enough for me to break the old belief.

I am sure that the sub teacher who insulted me was just frustrated herself. She was just human and had a bad day. I think that of my brother and of my grandmother. I was the one who let their emotion, thoughts, and words stay with me. I allowed them to be my beliefs when they were not meant to be. If you have a belief that doesn't make you feel good, if it doesn't help you and others, if it is unkind, or hurtful, then it isn't a belief that you want to keep.

Beliefs create our personality. Whether we are kind, or cruel, confident or insecure all stems from our beliefs. Author and neuroscientist Joe Dispenza said "Your personality creates your personal reality. A new state of being is a new personality. A new personality creates a new personal reality. Change your beliefs, change everything.

Here are a few of my favorite quotes about beliefs

1. "The outer conditions of a person's life will always be found to reflect their inner beliefs." James Allen
2. "To accomplish great things we must not only act, but dream: not only plan, but also believe. Anatole France

3. "Be brave to stand for what you believe in even if you have to stand alone." Roy T. Bennett

4. "Believe something and the Universe is on it's way to being changed. Beacause YOU'VE changed, other things start to follow. Isn't that the way it works?' Diane Duane

5. "It's not who you are that holds you back, it's who you think your not." Denis Waitley

6. "We live in a Universe that responds to what we believe" Corbin Henry

7. "Those who stand for nothing fall for anything." Alexander Hamilton

Affirmations for Changing Your Beliefs

Say these next sentences out loud:

"I am open minded and open hearted to new Ideas."

"I am open minded and open hearted in all areas of my life."

"I now accept positive change in all areas of my life."

"I love myself, I accept myself."

Now go back and say these affirmations once again. Did you do it? Okay, now say them one more time.

Now I want you to write those four sentences down in your notebook. Or write them on a piece of paper and put it up next to the mirror in your bathroom. Every time that you walk into the bathroom for the next thirty days, I want you to look yourself in the eyes in the mirror and say this to yourself. You may not fully believe these words at first, but you can "fake it until you make it."

CHAPTER 3

Failure – Path to Success

Failure can be one of those ego triggering button pushers. For some Failure is the ultimate defeat. They feel their life is over. If a task or situation didn't produce the desired outcome that we wanted, we consider ourselves a failure. Google says the definition of failure is lack of success, the omission of expected or required action. By knowing the second half of that sentence, I now understand one thing. Failure only happens when you quit. When you give up and decide that you aren't going to pick yourself up again then that is a failure. People become successful, because they never gave up, they never stopped trying. Morgan Freeman explains exactly what failure is and why it is so important for our human growth "Failures are apart of life. If you don't fail, you'll never learn. If you don't learn you'll never change."

Failure is change. We learn what works, and what doesn't.

It's inspiring to look at the lives of people who no one would ever have expected to make it to the top, or achieve all the goals and dreams that they dared to follow. They are the ones who remind us that anything is possible as long as we keep pushing forward and have a little courage to venture out into the unknown to places where others are scared to go. Let failure empower you, instead of defeat you.

Albert Einstein is one of the best examples. This genius didn't say a word until the age of four. He failed his entrance exams to the college he wanted to attend, he only passed the math and science. And he almost changed his career to an insurance salesman because his dad kept trying to get him a job, because he was afraid his son would always be a failure. Yet he still kept going after his goal of producing a useful physical theory and not taking no for an answer. Through his perseverance, he won a Noble peace prize in 1921 in Theoretical Physics, and his discovery of the law of the photoelectric effect. It wasn't the goal he had intended on, but that's still not bad.

Here is some of Einstein's wisdom to inspire your journey:

"Life is like riding a bicycle. To keep your balance, you must keep moving."

"No problem can be solved from the same level of consciousness that created it."

I like this one because, to me, he is talking about the ego. The ego mind is the one who created the problem, and therefore the ego won't be able to solve the problem. The solution will come from your soul, or higher mind. The soul will communicate with you, but you must make sure not to let your ego get in the way of your higher guidance.

Think about that for a moment. When problems arise in our lives, they are usually based on thoughts from the ego. For example: "I can't do my job right. I am going to get fired because they hired someone who knows more than I do."

Now, if you are saying something like that, you are actually causing yourself more problems. Once you affirm that you can't do your job right, your mind is going to do as it is told. If you say you can't, you won't. It's that simple. If you tell yourself, 'I am going to get fired,' many times, then you are really going to feel the energy of that. You will get fired because that will be the energy that you send out into the world. The law of attraction says that "like attracts like," and so this will be what you attract into your life.

So now that we understand the problems we create for ourselves with this ego mind, let's look at the soul mind which is the next half of the wisdom that Albert gives us. When Einstein says that you can't solve a problem from the same level, the higher level he means is the soul. Soul will come up in a gentle non-pushy way. It will be more of an "Ah ha" moment, and would give you the most obvious next move. If you are truly worried about someone coming in and taking your job because they know more than you, then you need to learn more. Take another class, read books or article – but do something. You have the choice to sit back and do nothing or you can step up and change the situation.

The next famous person I want to talk about is Oprah Winfrey. There probably isn't a person alive who hasn't heard of her. She hosts her own talk shows, started the tv network OWN, has published books (and a fabulous book club, by the way). She has more money than any lotto player could ever hope to win. She started out life struggling though. As a child she came from poverty and even suffered sexual abuse. Yet look at her now.

Here are some words of wisdom from this great woman:

"Breathe, let go and remind yourself that this very moment is the only one that you know for sure that you have."

"Turn your words into wisdom."

"Your journey begins with a choice to get up, step out and live fully."

Not everyone is an Oprah fan, but we can all learn from her example. She chose a path that helps others and she got rich from doing it! She came from a past that I know would cause many people to be consumed by bitterness and anger. But she overcame all that in her journey. The questions she asks in her interviews with spiritual teachers like Eckhart Tolle really dig in deep to get the understanding. I am often amazed when she asks many of the same questions I would.

Thomas Edison is a perfect example of perseverance. no matter how many times you fall down, you get back up and try again. When he was just a boy, he ended up having hearing problems after his ears were grabbed by the trainman who was trying to help him board. He was homeschooled. Edison is known for inventing the light bulb. He failed over ten thousand times, but he kept going until his experiment was a success. Whenever I think of the word perseverance, he is the one that comes into my mind.

Edison is famous for these words of wisdom:

"I have not failed. I've just found 10,000 ways that won't work."

This quote is posted on the wall in the cafeteria at my children's elementary school. I substitute teach at the school sometimes. Whenever I'm on lunch duty, I like to read this inspiring message before the kids come in. It reminds me that I haven't failed, when it comes to my goals and dreams, I just haven't yet found the way that will work for me. This should be a reminder for all of us. We only fail when we don't get back up, when we give up.

The story of Steve Jobs is a perfect mixture as far as showing both inspiration and over coming fear. He actually was afraid to fail. He dropped out of college and got kicked out of a business that he helped create. He didn't curl up into a ball and crawl into the corner though. He used his failure to help him grow and learn.

Steve Jobs said that he used the thought of death to over-come the fear. Now B has said something about using death to be a motivator too. For some that is pretty powerful – knowing that you don't have forever, and that tomorrow may never come. This can give you the push that you need. Personally, the thought just gets my heart racing, "Crap! I don't want to die tomorrow." I was amazed to learn that Steve Jobs studied with a guru.

Here are some words of wisdom from Steve Jobs:

"Being the richest man in the cemetery doesn't matter to me. Going to bed at night saying we've done something wonderful, that's what matters to me."

Let me tell you why I like this quote. I am not very good at setting goals and even worse at actually following through on them. A few years ago I needed to come up with a few goals. Some were easy: Make it a point to keep up on my hair. Cook dinner more often, and eat out less. But coming up with career and life goals was not easy. I have always wanted to do many things, because I enjoy learning and doing new things. So getting it down to one goal is something that I still can't do. My goal at one time ended up being to help seven million people in some positive way before I die (it started at seven hundred, but that wasn't big enough). Now I want to help seven-hundred million people as my ultimate life goal. I give smiles, I give advice, I offer help when I see a need. While it may seem like nothing, to someone else it might mean everything. I know that on my rough days, that one kind person made all the difference in the world to me. I went from feeling lonely to feeling connected by small, simple acts of kindness.

Steve Jobs is right when he say that we can be the richest person in the world, but if we aren't doing anything to help others, to contribute in some way, our souls will not feel fulfilled. We will just feel empty. We are meant to be of service in this world. That belief upsets some people because it threatens their ego. The ego is out for itself and no one else. The soul is out for others. That is a quick way to see in a situation whether you are operating from the ego or the soul. The ego will be wondering how it benefits, what you can get out of it. The soul just wants to help someone else, not wanting anything in return. The soul doesn't even want a thank you or acknowledgement from anything. It just wants to help. Steve Jobs was a very wise man.

For anyone who has a smart phone, you know that you can go into the app store and find apps for anything pretty easily. When I first started this new way of living, I needed more than just reading affirmations when I was at home. So I found a great app and had affirmations sent to my phone four times a day. I had over 200 affirmations and quotes coming to me each time.

Steve Jobs said something that was so powerful for me that I had it sent to me all four times. Every time I read it, I could hear his voice. Strangely, at the time, I had never heard what his voice sounded like. Months later, when I heard a recording of his voice, it sounded exactly as I imagined it.

This quote hits me someplace deep in my heart; maybe it's the part of me that is hidden, that wants to play small in life, and these words give it encouragement. Here is what he said: "Life can be so much broader once you discover one simple fact, and that is that everything around you that you call life was made up by people who were no smarter than you and you can change it, you can influence it."

When you look at something through these eyes, of course you would open up to your own full potential, of course you would believe in yourself. The only difference between the people who succeed and those who don't is that those who succeed never give up. You are not the only one struggling, Some of these people took years to make a name for themselves. But they never stopped. We always want fast results, but that is not what we are meant to have. We are meant to be knocked down and have failures; that way, we get up stronger. We are meant to get the "dents," as Mater from the Disney movie "Cars" would say, and we are meant to keep them, not buff them out. Each dent tells a part of our story. When you fall down and get dented it is just another chapter in your human life book, and another soul experience.

Will Smith is yet another amazing man who I have so much respect for. I admire him for his acting, marriage, and his wisdom. He has so much truth and love to share in this world that we all need to stop and listen to him. Will Smith plays a role in the movie, *Collateral Beauty* that was a perfect fit for him.

He writes letters, as a form of therapy, to Time, Love, and Death – and they answer him! Anyone reading this needs to buy this movie and a box of tissues. Witness the power of writing letters to heal our wounds.

He is now an inspirational and motivational speaker, a champion in the game of life on all levels, and another brave soul who never stayed down.

Here are some incredible words of wisdom from Mr. Will Smith:

"If you are not making someone else's life better, you are wasting your time. Your life will become better by making other people's lives better."

"Love is the ultimate theme but it's not just for women" (yes, he is saying for all humans).

"We spend money that we don't have, on things that we don't need, to impress people who don't care."

"The first step is that you have to say that you can."

The next quote from Will Smith is by far my favorite and was the most life-changing:

"You have to decide what you want to represent." He goes on to say that he "wants to represent possibility."

Thank you for that advice, Will. If we all would stop and ask ourselves that one simple question before we went out into the world each day, imagine how we could change things.

Each of us fails and makes mistakes. It is just what is going to happen. Bernadette taught me that in order to master something, I must first be willing to fail at it. Let me make it clear –

I do not like to fail. Everything in my chart is a one, my life path included, I like to be number one.

I have since accepted that I am going to fail and now I even give myself permission to fail which takes so much pressure off of myself I highly recommend that you say this "I give myself permission to fail" before doing any task. Kids make a lot of mistakes. They are just trying to learn what works and what doesn't work the same as all of us; they just have less experience in doing so. Failing is hard, there is no denying that but it's going to happen. Could you imagine how bored your soul would be here if everything that it did the first time it did right. Where is the learning in that? Your soul did come here to learn so that way it can grow. You are meant to learn until the day that you die. That is why the soul has it's journey here. That's why most of us are drawn to goals, and bucket lists (mine is a book, it's so long). So if your soul is here to learn then why do we get angry or upset with ourselves and others when a mistake is made? They just found a way that didn't work.

We now laugh about the mistakes we make in our house. If someone messes up dinner we laugh. When my sis in law ran into my parked car with the big red nose, antlers and a tail (it was Christmas time) we laughed at the insurance company. When you make a mistake, you are either going to laugh about it or cry about it. If you laugh you give your soul permission to make mistakes and allow it to keep learning.

The Human can learn from books, hearing, watching. But the soul can only learn by doing and experiencing. The ego is the one that says it has to be the best, you can't fail – or if you fail, you suck. Tell the ego: "That's one way of looking at it. But I chose to look at it this way." And let the rest go.

Here are some other memorable quotes by various wise people

1. You must be the change that you wish to see in the world. – Gandhi

2. Do not be afraid of greatness. Some are born great, some achieve greatness, and others have greatness thrust upon them. – William Shakespeare

3. The master has failed more times than the beginner has even tried. – Stephen McCranie

4. Patience is the calm acceptance that things can happen in a different order than the one you have in mind. – David G Allen

5. To be angry is to let others' mistakes punish yourself. – Buddha

6. What we think we become. – Buddha

7. How people treat you is their Karma, how you react is yours. – Wayne Dyer

Affirmations on Failure:

1. I always succeed because I keep moving forward.

2. I have a success mindset, I believe in myself.

3. I am capable of achieving my goals.

CHAPTER 4

Forgiveness A Master Key

Forgiveness is one of those master keys to living the human life. Forgiveness is making the conscious choice to release any negative feelings toward a person, group or situation who has caused you hurt or pain. It doesn't matter whether they deserve to have forgiveness or not. Forgiveness isn't saying what they did was right, or that you have to now forget it all, it doesn't mean that you have to allow them back into your life or that you shouldn't peacefully let someone go. Forgiveness is for you. It is releasing yourself from suffering.

It is very hard to put into words and the action I would say that I put right with it is forgiveness is accepting. I figure that I have forgiven everyone now. it took longer to forgive some more than others but I have since forgiven all. I figure that is where unconditional love comes in, where no matter what they do we are willing to forgive them and not hold the dreaded grudge against them (which really is a form of self hate in my opinion). If you're not ready to go to unconditional love go into unconditional forgiveness. When someone makes you mad go ahead and say "I feel ..... But I am willing to forgive you. Then peace and release letting it flow out like hot grease until the unpleasant feelings go away.

Forgiveness is the same thing. If you believe that you can't forgive someone for something that they did, then that belief will give you a lifetime of pain. The Buddha said, **"Holding onto anger is like drinking poison and expecting the other person to die."** Some say that when you don't forgive, the only person who gets hurt is you. I think that is half true. No, the other person is not hurting the way that you are. But when you have that energy, that pain, the belief that you can never forgive them, you will hurt others. When you trap that energy inside of yourself, it will even affect the ones you love the most. Your belief will control your actions and will flow out into all areas of your life.

When you don't forgive, you are also giving them your power because they are taking over your thoughts. If they hurt you, they were hurting inside too. You just don't know why, and you don't need to, but you don't have to be the one to hold them accountable for what they did. Let karma do that.

Letter for Releasing...

The bible says that we must forgive in order to be forgiven. We have all made mistakes, we all need to be forgiven by someone. Forgive yourself, forgive others just by simply saying, "I am willing to forgive you and let you go now." You don't have to say it to them, you just have to say it in your mind. If you feel like you need to give this person a piece of your mind, then write a letter, and burn it. The smoke will get your message out.

But at the end of that letter, be sure to write:

"I am willing to forgive you."

"I am choosing to forgive you because I choose to have peace for myself.

"I am choosing to take back my power and in order to do that, I have to forgive you, so I am willing to forgive you for all that you have done."

Don't wish anything bad on them, don't put any spells or curses on them. When you think of them, send them a ball of loving energy saying, "I hope you get the help you need, I hope you get your healing." That way, when you think of them, it is no longer negative energy you're sending out but positive energy.

I know many of you must be thinking, Why on Earth would I want to send them any kind of loving energy? It's simple: what you send out, you will get back. If you are still angry with them and you send out negative energy every time you think about them, then you'll attract that same negative energy into your life. It may show up at work, with family, friends, money, or in sickness. You don't know what role it is going to play in your life. But you can be sure that it won't be a good one. It will only bring you more heartache, more suffering, and more problems. Forgiveness is a step that we have to take towards freedom. It can end wars, bring people together, and bring joy into our hearts and lives.

So now you may be thinking, 'Okay, fine. I have to forgive. But, what does that mean? Am I supposed to let this person back into my life after all they have done?' If that is what forgiveness looks like to you in that situation, then I would say, yes. But a lot of times that is not the case. If it is someone that you want to keep in your life, like a spouse or your children, then of course tell them, "Hey, I love you and I forgive you." Plain and simple. By contrast, if it is someone from your past who you don't ever want to have in your life, then write a letter and burn it. Don't write a letter that says only the negatives. Yes, you can let that out, but don't focus on that. Instead, think of why they would do whatever it was. Something inside of them, a belief or an emotion caused them to act like that. If they said something about your parenting, maybe it was because they knew deep down that they were making bad choices as a parent. If they called you a bad spouse, it was probably because they felt like a bad spouse themselves. Oftentimes, when we come into contact with people that lash out at us, it is because something inside of them is broken. It can actually have nothing to do with you. They are just so wrapped up in their own drama that they lash out at others. Sometimes it can create the mirror effect – you are just holding up a mirror to reflect everything they are saying. They are basically talking to themselves, about themselves. It can sometimes trigger issues inside of us that we do need to work on. Our vibe attracts our tribe. If you are feeling negative energy inside of you, it's going to show up outside of you as well.

One of my clients had to let go of some deep painful issues through forgiveness. When she looked into the situation from childhood, she realized that even though she and her siblings had grown up in the same house, their stories were different. Her story was a beautiful one filled with love and joy. Whereas theirs were filled with abandonment and pain. They held onto this energy into their adult years with false beliefs; which made them do horrible things. My client/friend couldn't understand how they could do such things. She felt that they needed to pay for their mistakes. Her anger kept her in a dark place. One that hurt herself, her family, and her friends. She had health problems as well. When I first suggested the idea to her to forgive them, she freaked out. "Hell no!" were her exact words. So, I backed off. But every month I would bring up the subject whenever she asked me what to do about it.

We battled this way for months. Eventually, I showed her a video on Bernadette Logue's "The Daily Positive" website, called, "When, Why, and How to Forgive." Bernadette explains it in a way that I can't. It's so beautiful. My client/friend had an ah-ha! moment watching it. A few days later, she wrote a letter to her siblings, and made a YouTube video about letting them go. About two weeks later, her spirit was still higher. She said she had felt the difference the moment she did the process.

It took me a few years to write my own letters to the people I needed to forgive. First, I was ready to forgive. Then, I got to a place where I needed to apologize for the hurtful things that I had said, because I had screwed up, too. My client wanted nothing to do with the whole apology thing. I encouraged her to have compassion; that their story was different. I also suggested, as in my own letters, to thank them for even one thing that they taught her or did for her. In her video, she apologized that their stories were different. And she thanked them for being there and cheering her on when she used to sing on stage. In the same video, she giggled over the happy memories. She kept repeating, "I have to let you go now." She ended the video with burning the letters. It was beautiful to see her finally at peace.

The letters that I wrote have not been burnt. They are sitting in the glove box of my car waiting for the day when I am ready or brave enough to mail them out. Just writing them though shifted my energy enough that I don't even get triggered anymore by the sound of their names. As with my client, the power these people once had over me is now gone.

By forgiving, you change the belief. Where you once believed that you had to hold them accountable for all of their actions, you now realize that they were acting out their own karma through a higher power than you personally have. They will get the effects from that. Don't make their karma your karma. You have your own to deal with. Why add more to it than you need to?

Many years ago, I was over at my parents' house enjoying our weekly Friday night dinner with my family. Yes, I know – sort of "Gilmore Girls," but we care about each other. And we made it a point to get everyone together. We valued that time. I don't remember what started the conversation, but the moment I heard the name Anna, I was infuriated. Anna and I had a falling out a few years before and I had not forgiven her. I went off telling my dad how much I hated her and wished her dead. I could feel my face turning the color of a beet with all my energy trapped in me. I am my father's daughter. Just like my dad when he gets fired up, he says things he shouldn't say or really doesn't mean. But in that moment, you don't stop. You just go off until you find the tools to help you handle things in more constructive ways.

At the time, I was still in destructive mode. However, my dad was meditating and having weekly sessions with his Gasha (he was one of seven English speaking monks.) and reading books about meditation and enlightenment. It was fun to talk to him about this stuff. I always talked with my grandpa about God. But my dad was the one who knows a lot about spiritual things, religions, cultures,...and the Dalai Lama. Whether my dad liked it or not, we could always tell the times when he had been working on meditation that week and when he hadn't. He had this wise sense of peace about him on the days that he met with his Gasha. He shared a piece of information that Gasha taught him. "How do you fight hate?" he asked me. I am sure, while in destruction mode, that I said something like, "A weapon."

Before he spoke, he shook his head. "No, you fight hate with compassion." This was so profound for me – an epiphany. It was the first piece of advice and the lesson that got me started on the path of my spiritual journey. My dad did not speak to me that day. My dad's soul spoke to my soul in a way that I didn't comprehend. He reminded me who my soul was when I had forgotten. I did not forgive her that day, by the way. It took me another three years to do so. And then another two years to write the letter that now sits in the glove box of my car.

The day that I wrote her that letter was the day I knew I had truly let her go. I had moved through the normal stages – or at least, it seemed normal to me. I got to a place of not calling her names. Then not saying bad things about her. Then I began praying for her, and then seeing that she was just hurting, too. Her last text message to me said she "would pray for me." Now, there is a difference between someone praying for you (love, kindness, hope you get better, etc.) and someone using that as a hidden way of saying, 'You're messed up in the head and need fixing.' When she had said that to me, I knew it was the second case. Though when I got to the compassion stage, I thought, 'What if she really had prayed for me and God listened to her prayers?' So in the letter, I thanked her. (Someone texted me while writing this book to tell me that Anna had cancer. Perhaps the person was curious to see how I would react. Instantly, I felt compassion for her, for her family, and prayed for her.) I hope that she will heal, her family needs her.

She wasn't all bad, just lost like I was. If I had learned about forgiveness sooner we could have been friends. A regret that I had to forgive myself for.

Another question that may come up for you about forgiveness is this:

Why do I even need to forgive to get rid of my old beliefs? Can't I just skip this step? Well, you could, but then to some degree you will always have pain and suffering. You will have more negative emotions than positive ones. The events in your life will never be what they truly were meant to be. You can't fully love anyone until you have completely forgiven everyone else. Including yourself. I know that some of you are thinking, 'Oh no, I can't forgive myself. Not with all the... I have done.'

All of us have a past. The past doesn't define you; it just shows you where you have been. The challenges you've gone through, the mistakes you have made, and the lessons that you have learned. Keep the lessons so that you can move forward to the next lesson. Give yourself compassion for doing the best that you could. You have to love yourself in order to love others. People may think of you as a good mom or dad. You may love your kids very much. But if you don't love yourself, then you can't possibly give them the amount of love you're capable of.

No one can tell you how long it will take you to fully forgive someone, my advice is take it take it slow, work on it daily.

Ho'oponopono

Ho'oponopono is an ancient Hawaiian tradition. It is a form of prayer, confession, repentance, restitution and forgiveness.

Ho'oponopono means to make things right. In the Hawaiian dictionary it is known as Mental cleansing. The Hawaiian historians believe that if you were sick it was because you had broken some kind of Spiritual law. They believe that the only way to be cured is to seek forgiveness from the gods because they were the only ones who could really heal you. They would also bring in a Kahuna or healer into the home as a mediator for the whole family giving the family a type of therapy.

In 1976 a Hawaiian healer named Morrnah Simeona found a way to modify the Ho'oponopono so that everyone would experience the healing benefits without someone entering for you. It has proven to have a powerful healing effect. This modified way combines the original version with karma. A therapist in Hawaii named Dr. Hew Len worked a long side her. He also went on to use this method when he worked for the Hawaii state penitentiary curing whole ward of insane inmates. He would read through the inmates files and take responsibility for whatever was going on in his inner world that was causing this outer world problems, and it worked!

Dr. Hew Len believes we should all take responsibility for things going on not just in our homes and families but also in the world at large. The prayer that he says requires us to use repentance, forgiveness, gratitude, and love. He believes when used together they have great power.

Here is the Ho'oponopono and you say it like this:

1. I'm Sorry (If you are taking responsibility, then you have to say you're sorry.)
2. Please forgive me (Say it and mean it.)

3. Thank you (Be thankful for everything you have, for every breath you take.)

4. I love you (Say it to your Creator, say to your inner divine self, say it to your body. Say it to your challenges because they help you grow.)

This is a fast way to move into the vibration of forgiveness.

I know that some people have been put through hell by the actions of others that make it hard to forgive. You can choose not to forgive. That is your choice. However, you then need to remember that until you forgive everyone for everything, there will always be pieces inside of you that will hurt; pain that you will keep. I'm not telling you to forgive because that person deserves it. I'm telling you to forgive because you deserve it. You deserve to be free from pain.

CHAPTER 5

Acronyms to Live By

If you've ever had any form of psychological therapy, then you are probably familiar with Dialectical Behavior Therapy (DBT). DBT therapy helps to change unhealthy patterns of behavior. It gives you skills for emotional regulation and teaches you how to accept things by developing mindfulness.

DBT therapy also gives you lots of acronyms to help you remember what to do. Here are some examples. The first is IMPROVE.

I-M-P-R-O-V-E

Imagery: Imagine being in a place that is relaxing for you. It could be an imaginary place or somewhere you have been.

Meaning: Find out the meaning or reason as to why you are feeling the way you do. What is the lesson it gives you? What needs to be healed or changed?

Prayer: Pray to God, the universe, the creator. Or chant a mantra.

Relaxation: Take deep belly breaths, relaxing with each inhale and letting go with each exhale.

Vacation (a quick one): Take a quick break from everything. Walk outside for a moment if you can.

Encouragement: Empower yourself with your positive words. "I will get through this. This too shall pass. I can do this!"

This acronym IMPROVE is linked with both being human and our soul self. Your ego is constantly telling your brain what to focus on. Instead, we need to switch off the ego so the soul can come through. Prayer connects us with our Creator and allows the soul an opportunity to lead the way. The human part of you needs to focus on what you are doing, and it also needs your encouragement just as a child would.

Another acronym used for emotional regulation is PLEASE:

P-L-E-A-S-E

Physical illness [LL]: If you are sick, treat the illness. Either with rest or see a doctor if you need to. Don't make any decisions while you are sick. They are never clear headed.

Eating: Eat a healthy diet (Have you heard the term hangry? It's being angry and irritable because you haven't given your body the proper food that it needs.

Avoid mood-altering drugs: Drugs and alcohol need to be avoided, and taking medications that aren't prescribed for you.

Sleep: Getting the right amount of sleep is important – not too much and not too little. A regular sleep schedule is also helpful.

Exercise: Do exercise that is effective. Therapists recommend aerobic exercise such as walking, jogging, zumba, etc. I recommend yoga.

One of the first things that I ask when I talk to someone going through a difficult time is: "Have you eaten? What did you eat? And when?" Your human body needs food to fuel it. Think of a car. If you don't give it fuel, it's not going to be much use to you. Don't just eat a tub of ice-cream either. Give your body some protein, vegetables, and fruit. My go-to comfort food is a big, greasy cheeseburger with lettuce, onion, tomato, and avocado, smothered in ranch dressing! You know what is best for your body. Health food fanatics reading this may be freaking out. But for me, sometimes the best choice is to listen to what my body wants. Once I have eaten my comfort food, I am able to face my challenges with a clear head.

When we are sick or in pain, it's not us who does the talking to other people. It is our pain talking. We say and do things that we later regret. It is just better to take care of ourselves before we do that. If you are sick, please go to the doctor and get some sleep. Don't push yourself too hard during this time. If you don't take care of yourself when your body is warning you, it will make certain that you have some down time. You have to take care of you in order to help anyone else. I can't stress that enough.

D-E-A-R-M-A-N

This acronym is for developing the interpersonal skills we need for communicating more effectively with the people we come across on this Earth journey.

Describe your situation: "The story I am telling myself is…"
When you talk with others trying to explain your feelings or
what is going on, you don't want to go into the blame game.
"You don't listen to me, no one ever listens "are things that if
you say to someone they aren't going to listen to you, they feel
attacked and will become defensive. Instead you want to
describe what is going on, or what you are feeling. Remember
the thoughts are coming through as the story that you are
telling yourself so a more productive approach to your situation would be saying something like "The story I am telling
myself is I am not worthy of being heard, or I am all alone and
have to handle all this on my own." Another way is "you know
this is hard to do and I really need some help. There's a lot of
work to be done and it is more than one person can handle."

Express: Why is this an issue or problem for you? And say your
emotions, "I feel …."

Assert: Assert yourself by asking for what it is that you want,
"I would like ….

Reinforce: Reinforce your position by offering positive consequences.

Mindful: Be aware of the situation at hand. Keep your focus on
what you want, not what you don't want.

Appear: Look confident even when you don't feel it. Again,
fake it till you make it.

Negotiate: Don't hesitate with people; and both of you come
up with a compromise that you both can live with. Compro-

mising is something that we will always have to be willing to do.

Sometimes conversations with other humans can be hard. We all have our own agendas, wants, and needs. If you come at people with just emotion, then you are just going to be a mess when communicating. Your words may be aggressive; your mind may be foggy. It's okay to have emotions, but you also need to make sure that you are expressing them in the right ways.

Think of when you were a kid getting yelled at from your parents. If the conversation went on too long, did you shut them out or did you still listen to them? What about if they talked with you when they were calm, did you listen better? Did things get resolved from yelling or talking? People are more likely to hear and understand you when you aren't trying to point fingers. That is why "the story that I am telling myself" is a great way to get out your emotions without someone else shutting them down.

G-I-V-E

The next one I will share with you is for you to use in your relationships with your spouse, family, friends, and co-workers. We tend to be the hardest on our family because we feel that we can get away with more. They are our family, so sometimes in our minds we think that they have to take our bad days, our dramas, and our extra baggage. While it is nice to have such loving and supportive people in our lives, it is also nice to treat them the way we would our best friend. So put extra work in this one to help get along with the ones that are most special in our lives: GIVE.

Gentle: Use kind words. Avoid any kind of abuse; both physical and verbal (name calling, judgments or sarcasm; no put downs).

Interested: Act interested in what is being said to you. Listen with the intent of learning what someone is trying to tell you, with understanding (eye contact, questions, being present not distracted).

Validate: Show compassion and understanding for what they are going through; the story they are telling themselves. You don't have to agree with what they are saying, but you do need to acknowledge their pain/suffering.

Easy manner: breathe, be calm.

Even if you have never gone through what someone else has, you can look at them and see that they are hurting. You can hear it in their voice. You can see it in their actions. Put yourself in their shoes. If this had happened to you, how would you want someone to treat you? What would you want to hear?

Sometimes people don't want to hear any advice. Sometimes the best thing that you can do to help someone is by stopping what you are doing. Look them in the eyes and just let them get whatever it is off their chest. Don't say to them, "I told you so." Just validate them. "That must suck...that sounds painful...I'm sorry that you are going through this."

Sometimes when I am hurting or feel upset, all I want is for someone to give me five minutes to release it; to hear me and just say that they are on my side. For me, I want to feel like I am not alone in what I am facing. Having that support will make it release just as fast as it came, rather than dwelling on something.

A-C-C-E-P-T-S

This acronym is for the challenges that life tends to give us.

Activities: Use positive activities or hobbies. (go paint, fish, write, read, etc)

Contribute: Help others, volunteer.

Comparisons: Compare yourself to those who have it harder than you do.

(if everyone puts their problems into the fire, chances are you are going to want yours back)

Emotions (change to positive): try to laugh; laughter really is the best medicine.

Push away: temporarily focus on something else; come back to it later.

Thoughts (change): Make yourself think of something else.

Sensations (change): Do an activity that changes the sensations in your body; jump in the pool, eat spicy foods, pet the dog, etc.

Acceptance is such a hard task for us humans. We think we know best, and that things have to go our own way, when we say, how we say – or else we'll fail and it will be the end of the world. When we are down a dark hole, it can be tough to see the light. By learning these skills, our human self can learn that it's not always up to us. Volunteering is one of the best ways to learn how to accept. For one thing, you are helping someone else. For another, your mind is focused on something else. You allow space into the situation that you are struggling with. And you allow yourself time to come up with a solution, or maybe give yourself the time to heal. Either way, it benefits you and all of those around you. Even if you can't see it yet. Acceptance is hard, but not impossible.

The next two acronyms will help you maintain self-respect: FAST and THINK.

F-A-S-T

Fair: Be fair to you and others. What solution is fair to all?

Apologies: Apologize only once for something that was done ineffectively.

Stick to your values: Stay true to what you believe (see belief is important)

Truthful: Don't lie. It only causes more problems. Don't make webs of lies. Instead, plant gardens of beautiful truths.

T-H-I-N-K

Ask yourself these questions before you say anything:

Is it **T**ruthful?
Is it **H**elpful?
Is it **I**nspiring?
Is it **N**ecessary?
Is it **K**ind?

If you get a "NO" to any of these questions, then don't say it.

F-E-A-R

Along my Journey, I met a wonderful woman who is both a minister and a life coach. We will call her Martha. I had been digging deeper and handling difficult emotions for probably four years at this time. I was especially dealing with fear and anxiety. I remember sitting in her cozy office trying to explain something I couldn't understand. I had no explanation for the fear and worry going on. All I knew was that it made my heart race and my stomach turn, and I didn't like it. She shared a very logical explanation with me. I started crying because I was confused about the thoughts that were going on in my mind. She stood up and walked over to her desk, grabbing a piece of paper and a pen. Then she sat back down in front of me with a smile and wrote the word FEAR to describe what fear really is:

False

Evidence

Appearing

Real

You see, when the mind and body get that energy trapped inside, bottled up, as we say, you will take only about 20% of what you see before jumping to a conclusion that is based on past events. So, if the situation was a negative one, it is making the mind and body relive that event even if it isn't what is really happening. Your heart can race. You feel sick. Most likely you are in fight-or-flight or freeze mode. Your body thinks it is doing the right thing. It's trying to protect you. If you are in a situation where you really are in danger, please get away.

Learn to know the difference between a perceived danger created by our mind/beliefs and a life-threatening situation where you truly are in danger.

After seeing Martha that day, I wrote F.E.A.R. on my hand every day for a week, and anytime I felt that anxiety and fear coming up, I just repeated to myself, "False evidence appearing real." The only danger I was in was the danger I was causing to myself. The mind is meant to be used as a tool, but it's not supposed to be used against you. Its purpose is to help you observe and process the world around you.

Recently, I visited Sensay at her mom's house, just up the road from me. The house is beautiful, both inside and out. It's a tranquil Zen-filled oasis that I get excited about visiting every time that Sensay invites me over. The moment I walk in the door, I am greeted with a warm welcome, like family. I get to soak up the peaceful energy that flows through the space of this beautiful house. My Sensay, her mom, and I were in the kitchen talking while Sensay made me the most delicious chai tea (it was my first time trying it and a new experience for my soul), the best that I had ever had. As I sat down at the counter getting ready to do a candle wax reading for her, we were talking about the mind. Her sweet mom got an "ah ha" look on her face, and quietly walked off to her room while Sensay and I kept digging into the strange ways of the mind.

Moments later, she returned with a book called, *The Divine Matrix*, by Gregg Braden. Now, we were supposed to read this book together, but I was so fascinated by it that I couldn't stop reading. Some of the information wasn't new to me, such as the fact that we're all connected. I knew that very well. But Braden reinforced my understanding with new ideas and ways of looking at it that I hadn't considered before. One of the things that really stood out for me was the way he described fear. Braden said that fear is derived from three things: abandonment, self-worth, and lack of trust.

When you really stop to think about that, it makes sense. If I am worried that my spouse is going to leave me, doesn't that fall into all three of those things? If I am worried that I am going to lose my job, is that not lack of trust and self-worth? So maybe it's time to challenge those fears. Find out why you have them and release them as they come up. Ask yourself, Why do I have this fear? Is it because I don't feel worthy of love and companionship? Is this a belief that I have? Go back as far as you can in your memory and see what comes up that you picked up this belief. Challenge it by asking, What is another way that I can look at this situation? For example: "Well, if I lose my job, then maybe I could go back to school or go for that dream job, because now nothing is holding me back."

In the emotion of fear there are lessons to be learned, or skills to master. Whenever I try something new, there's always a piece of me that feels fear because I don't know how to do it. It's a beautiful mixture of fear and excitement, but shame often hides inside of it. I am always worried that I am not going to be good at something, or that I might fail in front of others. Shame is not a subject that people want to talk about.

Research professor and author Brené Brown explained it in a way that I find helpful: "Shame is the intensely painful feeling or experience of believing that we are flawed and therefore unworthy of love and belonging – something we've experienced, done or failed to do makes us unworthy of connection." What a wise, wonderful person to word it that way. I do believe that fear and shame do go hand in hand.

What I have learned about fear, shame, self-worth, and abandonment is that when you dig deeper, you'll find a belief that is centered around love. We may have a fear that we aren't lovable, or that we have done something so horrible that we are no longer worthy of being loved. Or maybe we think that if we are ashamed, then people won't love us anymore. If we were abandoned, we may feel that it was our fault and no one will ever love us. None of this is true. It's just your mind trying to give a story to how you are feeling, using past memories as the "proof" that what you're going through now is the same and will have the same ending as before.

Using Your Values

If you haven't already please go back and write down each one of these acronyms in your mini notebook before moving to the next part of this chapter. Don't just have them sit in your notebook. Use them, read them, practice them. Practice until it just becomes second nature to you.

Also take the time now to think about your values. What do you value? Write them down.

I value…. Try to write down seven things that you value. Here are mine:

I value my kids and being a good mom.

I value my husband and being the best spouse that I can be.

I value my family.

I value my friends.

I value my health in mind, body, soul (including God and my spirituality).

I value fun and adventure.

I value learning.

Next, write down your happy thought that makes you smile or laugh. Think of it like Never Never Land when you are there. You find your happiness though you are able to do impossible things like fly. If you think about what your happy thought is before you are triggered, you can have it written down. That way when you are in the moment of destruction, you can take out your little book and remind yourself what that happy thought is, who or what it is, and you can change the emotion and the thoughts that you are having. Often times our happy thoughts and our values are intertwined together.

My happy thought is my kids. For example, we have a video of our daughter the first time she tried anchovies. She was trying to gross out her brother, who was standing there saying, "Ewww." She says, "Oh man, I am in love with my mouth!" as she shoves in the cracker with the tiny piece of cream cheese and a little fish on top. The next moment, she gags and runs off to the trash can. I crack up just telling this story now. I can stand in a room by myself and think of that and instantly start laughing. It has never failed me. Though it can make for some awkward situations. One day I was in an empty classroom cleaning up, and when one of the other subs came in to talk to me I was standing there laughing for no apparent reason. (True story). Since I value being a mom, I am able to use my happy thought to pull my mood into a positive one at any time.

Emotions are not who you truly are at a soul level. Emotions are an experience that your body is feeling in a physical way. The emotions were produced by a thought that you had. The energy from that thought spread, throughout your body, and now you are feeling the emotion physically. Sometimes you may feel this as a stomach pain or butterflies, or a headache. It may show up as chest pain or your heart racing,

Whether they are good or bad, positive or negative, emotions are still just a passing feeling that in ninety seconds time is going to be gone. Anything after that ninety seconds comes from the thoughts you have, and a thought is just a thought. Anything more is just based on a judgment that you gave to your experience in that moment.

Sometimes it can be hard to know who we truly are because we associate our feelings and the roles we play in this world with our self – it's not who we really are, who our soul is. When you have a problem going on and you feel down about something, do you say, "I *am* sad?" or "I *feel* sad?" Do you see the difference? It's the same thing to watch for when trying to correct our children from a behavior that we don't approve of. If you always tell the child that they "are bad," they will believe they are bad. Instead, as parents we can tell the child: "That was a bad choice." That way he/she can associate the "bad" with the action they made, or with the behavior and not turn it into "I am a bad boy or I am a bad girl."

The same holds also true when your kids bring home their report card. When they hand it to you and they got straight A's, you want to tell them, You are so smart! (I've done it myself, no judgment here.) Instead, we need to point out how hard they worked to get those grades. That way if/when they get a bad grade, they won't pick up the belief such as 'I am dumb.' Instead they can look at the grade and say something like, I need to study more, or do extra credit or whatever their sweet little brains give them for a positive solution. I tell my kids that I don't expect straight A's from them. If they always had straight A's, what would be the point in being in school? You already know everything.

My husband has a great saying that he tells me anytime I see him lost in thought, pacing around the house. When I ask, "What's your problem?" he will say, "I don't have problems, I only have baby solutions." I love that he looks at life that way. It is a positive belief that he has cultivated. It keeps his mind from going into destruction mode, keeps it on the task at hand and allows him the open mind to find the solution to his challenges.

PART TWO

Let's Get Down to the F.A.C.T.S.

CHAPTER 6

F is for Metaphysical Facts

F

F is for factual information. Google says that a belief is "an acceptance that a statement is true, or that something exists" it is also "Trust, faith, or confidence in someone or something"

I of all people understand that when your confidence is down it is really tough to believe good things about yourself. We all came here as a soul, our soul came from somewhere. Your soul has certain truths that no matter what you do it still exists and can never be taken away. We're born/come in with unique qualities and alignments and that astrology, numerology, Akashic records give us "facts" give us a map of about who we are, and help us with our challenges, and our life purpose. These facts are not the same as facts about history, what town you live in, what your body looks like etc. These is cosmic, divine information. So F really must stand for more than factual information, more like metaphysical or spiritual information. You find out who your soul is. We are all made up in a different way. We see things differently and we react differently and the way that we are each designed is also different.

The Human design is a good place to start with this. Ra Uru Hu is the founder of The Human design system. He uses different components such as science, astrology, and other ancient methods to establish how each one of us come into the Earth, and the reactions that we will have to the challenges we face.

When you find a trusted website or app for human design you can learn what your response to life is, the parts that you play, what soul profile you have which tells some of the roles that we play, what our conscious mind may think.

When you find a website that you like you will receive what is called a "profile" and it will show you the challenges you may face, how you respond to those challenges, how the world sees you, and how your emotions can be.

I for example have a 2/5 profile which means that I show up in this world the way that people need me to. I respond to the world with undefined emotions, which means that sometimes I pick up other peoples emotions and take them on as my own.

My husband is always amazed when we go into a store and people come up that I don't know telling me about a challenge they are going through. I offer some words of wisdom or a tool for them to use. Their energy then changes into one of hope; they laugh with me and end up hugging me at the end. Sometimes these strangers end up becoming my friends. Over the years I have grown used to it and welcome the opportunity to offer help.

For a long time, I didn't know why people would come to me out of the blue, and I did my best to block it from happening because I didn't understand it. After my Sensay taught me that it was because I was helping people deal with their karma, I was able to accept this role and see it as an opportunity to help. On the flip side, this doesn't always come up in a positive light either. Some of the karma that I help others deal with can be painful on my end, taking the brunt of the mean words or negative actions. The way I see it now is I have to keep my karma good, not create more.

Human design can also explain how you are in the world. It can teach you about who you are, and who you think you are. It can show you what strategy you use when life gets hard. So mine is I am reacting. Yep, I agree.

I am a reactor. When a challenge comes my way, I react and respond. If I am not being my true self, then I am reacting out of frustration. Those are very dark times when that happens – not just for me, but for those on the other end of my volcanic mouth. Sensay taught me how I came in using the energy of the Sacral Chakra which is what is consider my authority. It is the chakra responsible for the reacting. This explained a lot, since my root chakra and my sacral chakras tend to get blocked. I found out how my type is a Generator and how people like me can use the law of attraction to really move forward with our goals.

So, what type of design are you? Maybe you are a generator like me, or a projector, a reflector, or a manifestor.

Numerology

You find your life path number by adding your birthday together example – let's say the birthday we are looking for is 3-11-2001 then you break it up 3+ 1+1+ 2+ 0+0+1 = 8. It is similar to astrology; it uses numbers to see connections in a divine way to life. It is a belief that there is a mystical relationship between a number and one or more coinciding events. It is also the study of the value of letters to words and names to ideas. Numerology shows us our personality traits, our wishes, desires, soul numbers. It can give you insight into your day, week, month, year even your whole life. It explains the challenges you have, the gifts that you bring here, the lessons to learn, the relationships that you will have, even potential health problems. It is not evil, or bad or even scary. Numerology just gives you more tools to put in your tool bag to help you understand who your soul is and what your purpose is for being here. It helps you grow on a spiritual level.

Go find your life path number, your soul urge number, even your lucky number and let them guide you. Find the good qualities that your number possesses and write them down in the form of an affirmation. For example, I know that I am a life path number 1. Looking at that, I can see the qualities that the one life path number has, such as being a leader. So I would write:

"I am a good leader, or I am an amazing leader. I have the ability to lead others in a positive way." Something on those lines.

Number 1

1's in the positive are usually leaders and they are brave. If you are ever in a situation where you need courage, you can remind yourself that *I am brave.* You could also say *I have the ability to lead others in a positive way.*

1's are also very creative, and independent they make great entrepreneurs.

Number 2

2's are very sincere in their actions and they are cooperative. They are also adaptable, so if you are a two and want to go through changes or challenges more easily, you may try saying this affirmation: *I adapt to changes easily.* It reminds you of the truth of who you are.

Number 3

3's are very happy and joyful beings. They help bring the fun into the world. So for you, an affirmation may be: *I am happy and outgoing.* You also have a large amount of artistic talent, so if you don't feel it flowing out of you, try affirming: *I allow my creative talents to flow from me freely and easily.*

Number 4

4's are logical and have an eye for detail. They know how to get things done in a productive and practical way. One of your affirmations may be: *I know exactly how to get this done and I chose to allow those ways to flow from me now.*

Number 5

5's are very quick thinkers. They can be given a task and they will be coming up with solutions in a matter of minutes. You could easily use one of these affirmations: *I am a problem solver, I can solve any problem. I can face whatever challenges life gives to me in a positive way.*

Number 6

6's are very loving and have a deep need to be of help and service to other souls. Some of your affirmations may include: *I enjoy serving others, the work I do is meaningful and helps others. I feel good about the contributions that I make.*

Number 7

7's are very good at researching and finding out new and different ways of doing things. They are also the ones who can draw us into things because they can be persuasive and charming. You may say one of these affirmations: *I know how to ask for what I want and need, I speak clearly. "I am resourceful and know that I have any answers I need, I can find them.*

Number 8

8's like power. They like to be powerful, and they like to hold powerful positions when it comes to their careers. They are powerful beings. You may affirm: *I am powerful, I feel my power, I use my power for good and help others see their power.*

Number 9

9's are very giving. Like the 6's, they like to be of service to others, helping them in any way they can. They are very selfless. If you are a 9 having a block, then affirm: *I am giving, I give of myself and I feel good when I am able to help others. I see that the world needs my kind heart.*

Now, most of the time, numbers over 9 are dropped down to a single digit. However, there are a few master numbers that are not dropped down and they are:

Number 11

11's are both the dreamers and deep thinkers. They spend a lot of time in their minds. But also, more often than not, they are more spiritual than the other numbers because of their strong intuitive abilities. If you are an 11 and are having blockages, try saying: *I know how to easily make my dreams my reality and I am capable of making that happen now.*

Number 22

22's are the most powerful number. They are the master builders of life. They are highly evolved and know how to manifest anything they want. They are the ones who find the most success in the world because they know to achieve it with little effort. If you are a 22 and have a block, affirm what you really are: *I am a master builder. I know how to go after what I want.*

Number 33

33's have been some of the greatest people in the world. Thomas Edison and Albert Einstein were both 33's. Einstein tried to teach us about things like how space and time are linked together, and thanks to Mr. Edison, we have the light bulb! 33's live at a higher vibrational level and want all of us humans to achieve this higher level as well. If you are a 33, you're probably not even reading this book, because you are so spiritually advanced. But if you are reading and you happen to have a block, then remind yourself: I *am here to help raise the vibration of others. I use my gifts to be the light for others.*

See what other ones you can find, there are so many. Numerology.com sends me a weekly email giving me my forecast for the week, and what challenges I may face. If you have that knowledge, then you can prepare yourself. You can simply remind yourself that: *In the face of any challenge this week, I will be the light and love that this world needs. I am willing to always find the positive in any challenge that I may face and know that I will easily find the best solution.*

The Soul urge

Along with the Life path number your Soul urge or Heart desire number is another important one to put in the book of you. It tells you what you like and dislike, and can be a guide to what motivates you, it can suggest what your purpose here is. It shows you what your true desires are, and can tell you about some of the hidden gifts that you have to share with the world. It can uncover talents and be a beneficial guide. It can be found on the internet, there is a calculator that uses the vowels in your full name at birth. Knowing this number is just another tool to help you along your path.

Your Lucky Number

If you already know this number that is great! If you don't know this, then go online and do a reading that tells you what your lucky number is and just start using it. I wanted a lucky number, so I did some research and found out it was 7. This made sense. On every car I have ever owned, there has been a 7 on my license plate, When I get food and it's really good, there is a 7 in the price I have to pay. Now I use this number 7 trick as often as I can as another tool to guide me.

Karmic Debt Numbers

Karma is know as action. Isaac Newton would call this cause and effect. For every action that you make a reaction is sure to come at some point. Since our bodies do not know the difference between time and space, the energy from any past lives is stored inside of us. If you did not learn the lesson before you died in a past life, then you carry that debt with you until it is paid. T Not everyone has a karmic debt number, but if you are like me, then you do. My karmic debt number is 19. This means that while I have the qualities to be a very good leader, I also lack confidence in my leadership skills, and can be afraid to lead others due to a fear of being bossy. I have no problem from being bossy in my family. But I see this issue come up in other areas of my life where it tends to cause a problem. This can at times be a lonely feeling and it is one that I bring on myself. My job is to overcome this fear. Another part is to give help to others and also allow others to help me.

There are actually only four Karmic debt numbers: 13, 14, 16 – and of course 19. I recommend for everyone to find out if they have a karmic debt number, and then just use it to help you grow stronger.

Astrology

Astrology is the study of the position and relationships of the sun, moon stars and other planets. It is studying them to judge how they will influence our human actions.

Another tool that you can implement is by using the Zodiac signs. You will find that astrology readings show you very similar traits to that of the numerology. You can also find out what crystals will best help your personal zodiac sign to get through challenges, what colors you should wear, or which crystals will bring more of into your life to help amplify your energy.

As an Aries, it's no surprise that the leader is what really stands out for me. It is my both my greatest strength and my greatest downfall – if I do not use it the way it is meant to be used.

Aries are also Confident and quick witted, but on the negative side they can also be quick tempered and selfish and impatient.

Taurus are very loving, nurturing and reliable, but they can also be resentful and possessive if they are in the negative.

Gemini are easy going, and adaptable to most any situations. If they are in the negative they may be superficial, anxious and even tense.

Cancer is a very emotional sign, they are protective of what they care about and have a good imagination. If they are in the negative they easily become moody, and over sensitive. They may have a hard time with change.

Leo can be very loving, kind and creative. If they are in the negative then they will be very bossy, and are known to hold a grudge.

Virgos are very shy, and like to keep to themselves. They are also very reliable and are good problem solvers. If they are in the negative they can be perfectionist due to their high expectations of themselves and others. They can also be an over worrier.

Libras are very sociable, they are the charmers. It is hard to resist their easy going attitude. If they are in the negative they can over indulge and have a hard time making decisions.

Scorpios are intuitive and can be forceful. They are very in tune with themselves and with the world around them. If they are in the negative they can be very obsessive and resentful.

Sagittarius's are very intelligent both book smart and common sense. They enjoy their freedom. If they are in the negative though they can be very superficial. They can also be careless in some of their actions.

Capricorns are very careful and think a long time before making almost any kind of decision, they really like to think things through. They are also very disciplined. If they are in the negative they can have a pessimistic attitude towards everything and are just flat depressed and miserable.

Aquarius's are the humanitarians of the zodiac. They are always willing to lend a hand, they have big hearts. If they are in the negative, they can shut down emotionally and become detached.

Pisces's are highly sensitive people, they can take things to heart and become offended easily. They are also very intone to how others feel and can be very compassionate. If they are in the negative they can become very secretive, making them looking like they are up to no good.

Akashic Records

The next way to find out who you really are at a soul level is by using the Akashic records. The Akashic records refers to an energy field where everything that has ever happened from any past life, present life situation, or future possibility are stored. You can find information on where your soul originated – such as the star systems and planets where your soul has been. The Akashic records can show you what "between lives" jobs your soul had, what energetic realm your soul came from, and the energy that you bring now onto the Earth. It can tell you what you are here to teach and what you are here to learn. Maybe you are here and you have a challenge that you are going through, or you don't understand why you picked up a belief that you have. It could be because of something that happened in a past life. Since there is no time and space in the spiritual realm, your body doesn't understand that this is a new life for your soul. It doesn't understand the difference between a memory and the Now either. So what that can mean is that you carried the energy from a past life over with you into this life. For example, let's say that in a past life you got your heart broken and you said, "I will never trust again." Now in this life you have deep issues with trusting someone. Maybe you've dug deep but could find no reason why you should have a certain belief. Then you could do a meditation that will guide you into one of your past lives, the one that is related to the issue that you are struggling with. Go back to the event and rewrite the ending. Instead of saying, "I will never trust again," imagine dusting yourself off and saying, *I will make it through this, I will find the love that is right for me.* Hold the images in your mind until you feel that the new belief has stuck. Then take that energy with you as you come back into this reality.

The Akashic records can also teach you who your soul family is. We all have two kinds of families. We have our human family that we are born into or create by getting married and having children. We also have the Soul family. These are the people we meet that we feel like we know from somewhere but can't pinpoint why or how we know them. They could be the ones who really *get* us and understand us on a level that most other people don't.

There is a wonderful meditation by Dakota Walker that I find amazing: *Calling in your Soul family.* It will help you to attract other souls that your soul knows. It invites them to come into your life. These souls may have similar challenges to what you are going through, or they may have overcome these challenges and are now here to teach you what they learned in a way that your soul will understand. They may be here to help you get through something or to push you to be your best self.

The Akashic records also hold the knowledge of what you specifically are here to learn: your life lesson, your soul theme, and what areas of your life it will show up in the most. Whether it's family, relationships, health, work, etc. It can also tell you how much of the lesson you've already learned – what percentage you have completed. Most of the people I come across when I read their records for them are about 30-40% of the way complete. Oddly enough, most of them are in their thirties. I wouldn't expect for them to be that far along. After all, we are meant to learn these lessons for the majority of our lives, and we are meant to help others reach the peace and wisdom that we eventually will attain.

There are other ways beyond what I've shared in this chapter to find out who you are and what your soul is here for on Earth. But with the tools I've given you, I encourage you to learn about yourself, and understand fully what cards you are bringing to the table. All the beautiful and wonderful qualities that you have and that others need to see and learn from. Be the investigator of your life. Make a soul plan. It starts by understanding what your soul is doing here in the first place.

Recommended reading: *Soul Mastery Accessing the Gifts of Your Soul* by Susann Taylor Shier. As you flip through the pages of this book you will know what sounds just like you and know at a deep level it's true.

I want you to use a notebook and on the front cover write your name and soul book after it.

Example: Sapphire's Soul book

On the inside cover I want you to write your birthday, place of birth etc.

Now I am not normally what you would call a fan of technology the reason being is I think people spend way to much time on it and not only does it destroy our brains but it also destroys that quality time that we have with the ones that we love because some people can't even be at the dinner table without it! But in this case we will use it as a tool to find out who you really are.

CHAPTER 7

A is for Affirmations

𝒜

Now you have put in hours of research, reading and googling to find out all about the magnificent soul that you are. Let's take this information and put it to good use to remind you of your truths. Grab some index cards or sticky notes and get ready to write down some affirmations.

Maybe you're wondering, what are affirmations? Affirmations are statements that you repeat to yourself to rewire your brain to get rid of old habits of thinking. Letting go of the negative thoughts allows room for the new ones. It is a tool used to help you create new beliefs and thoughts and, as a result, you create new actions. Affirmations work on both a conscious and subconscious level.

You may have found from your research that if you would just get past your insecurity that you could be a powerful leader for others.

Two time Oscar award winner Tom Hanks is a perfect example of this. His childhood consisted of him moving ten times before he even enter middle school. He had suffered from crippling shyness. Because of the divorce of his parents and the difficulties that brought on, he also felt very alone most of the time. In an interview he had, he explained that he often times felt insecure over his squeaky voice.

Here is a piece of wisdom from Mr. Hanks:

"Well, as with anything, if you want to believe you can find reasons to."

So on your paper write down that new belief. "I am a powerful leader." "I am confident and secure in who I am."

Decide where in your house you can put this affirmation so you will look at it every day. Now make another one and put it on the computer at your desk. You could get an affirmation app to have them sent to your phone or tablet.

You can also use your affirmations to help you with certain qualities that you want to have. Let's say that you have a live speaking event coming up where you will be standing on a stage in front of thousands of people; there that would be a terrifying prospect. But the solution isn't to find a way to get out of the event. The solution is to affirm that you are fully ready to handle this like a pro!

I am confident in my abilities

I have all the skills I need to be successful at this

The world needs to hear what I have to say and I will share it with clear, open communication

I accept that I feel fear but I am choosing to do this anyway.

I allow my courage to come forward now

Maybe courage and confidence aren't things that you struggle with. Maybe it's standing up for yourself at work. These affirmations would help you:

It is ok for me to stand up for what I believe in

I stand up and speak up for what is right.

I am heard and my wants and needs are recognized and valued

Perhaps you struggle with your weight or body image – a common issue that all souls will have to encounter at least once in their lifetime. Then you would work on accepting your body:

I accept my body.

I am choosing to see my beauty.

I am choosing to be comfortable in the skin that I am in.

I thank my body for all that it does for me.

I forgive myself for not being perfect.

I love myself just as I am

Anytime a challenge comes your way, you can flip it around. Rather than saying, "I can't," you say, "I can," and make an affirmation. Whatever negative thing you tell yourself, catch it and say, "That is my old belief and one that no longer serves me. I am letting that belief go now. Instead, I choose to believe this …."

If you wouldn't say it to your friend, don't say it to yourself. If you would say it to your friend and it is still hurtful, then you still shouldn't say it to anyone involved and should choose to be kinder. You have to watch what you say because you are listening to yourself. Whatever words you say about you and your life is the story you are creating right now.

If you find yourself struggling with money, what are your beliefs around money? Does money come easily or is it hard to come by?

What about other skills, such as cooking? Do you set off the alarms in your house every time that you cook? What are you telling yourself? Do you say my cooking sucks? If you are, then you are making it turn out that way.

Years back, my cooking was terrible. I didn't cook for enjoyment. I was just caring for my family. I did it because that is what I was supposed to do. Because I am the mom, and the captain of the household. I would hurry up to get it done and we would have a bowl or plate of slop. I actually liked cooking, but because I had a few failures with it when I was learning how to cook, I developed the belief that I was not a good cook. I wasn't someone who could just go from a negative belief to a positive one. I tried, but my mind fought too hard with me, causing an internal struggle.

Eventually, I learned to give myself permission to fail, and permission to be a lousy cook. No matter what, I was determined to add one ingredient to the meals I made, and that was love. What turned my attitude around was a story about a woman who used this magic ingredient in her cooking. The woman had this spice jar that she would shake over every single dish that she made for her family, then she would quietly put it back in the cupboard. Her mother had given her the shaker when she got married. The husband watched from a distance, wondering how that spice could go into every meal. He asked her about it one day after the kids had grown up and moved out of the house. But she would only smile, not answering his question.

When the woman became old and was unable to cook anymore, the husband took over.

"Remember to put the special spice in," she said from the other room. The husband didn't think much of it. He made them supper and brought it to his wife.

She took a bite. "You didn't put my spices in, did you?"

"No." he said "How did you know?"

She smiled but didn't answer. A few weeks passed and the husband was still cooking all the meals and the wife kept asking about her spice. Finally, one day, as the husband stood over the stove top, he grabbed the box that held his wife's spice. Pulling out the shaker, he saw the words written on the front: "Special spice – Love." Inside the box there was a note from the woman's mother saying that, with every meal, she should put in at least a few shakes of this spice to make it special for her family.

That story truly inspired me. And I do know how it changed me. I have an old saltshaker with the words "Love" written on the front. My husband smiles every time he sees me shaking it over whatever meal I am in the process of cooking. When I shake it, I say, "I love Branden (my hubby); I love Faith (my daughter); I love Chance (my son); and I love me." If I am making something such as a Thanksgiving or Christmas dinner, I do the same thing. Only the list of people that I love includes everyone who is coming to share that meal with us.

The other thing I say every time I try a new recipe is, "I give myself permission to fail at this, I give myself permission to completely suck at this."

I tell my husband about the new recipes. "So we are trying this tonight. It might be good, it might not. If it's not good, we'll go get a pizza."

My cooking has greatly improved. I know part of that is because I took the pressure off myself that I couldn't be human and make mistakes. Mistakes are how we learn and grow. It was the beliefs that I was telling myself that told me otherwise.

You can listen to affirmations that you can find on apps such as Headspace or you could even go on to YouTube. You can pop in some earbuds as you're drifting off to sleep. You don't have to stay awake to listen to them. Your mind will still hear them even as you sleep. There are some really good ones too that last the whole night for almost any situation or challenge that you are going through. When you put your makeup on in the morning, you can listen to them while standing in front of the mirror. Doing it this way has an added benefit – you can look into your own beautiful eyes and say them.

Affirmations can be streamed through Bluetooth in your car, and you can listen and repeat them as you drive to work. If you are at a job that allows you to wear headphones, then I say listen to them, but be aware of what is going on around you and make sure that you are safe but for me when I do it that way the thoughts in my head are silenced. My mind doesn't have time to run its own story because it is too busy focusing on what it is hearing as I am doing my normal daily tasks.

There are online meditations with beautiful pictures of nature on the screen. When you listen to affirmations while watching pictures on the screen, your brain magically picks up on this information.

Affirmations are in no way a quick fix for issues. You can't say them for a couple days and expect to see results. You also can't say them for a few weeks, start to change, and then stop, thinking that you no longer need them. It's a lifelong tool that you are choosing to give to yourself because you deserve to remind yourself just how amazing you are.

In Bernadette Logue's book, *Unleash Your Life*, she has pages upon pages of different affirmations that you can use until they become your new beliefs, your new truth. She also offers some amazing affirmation audios for all areas of your life.

I remember one day I was very frustrated with the fact that I had been doing the affirmations for a few weeks and I wasn't getting the result that I wanted. She told me to keep going with them anyway. So I did.

A few more weeks passed, and I began a task that I wasn't a hundred percent sure I was capable of doing. But that's when I heard Bernadette in my head, saying the very things to me that I had been listening to on her audios for so long. I took comfort in that, because it was like hearing from a friend. It was the pep talk that I needed.

When I took one of B's online classes called, "30 days to optimism," she would give us beautiful quick one-line mantras. I would read them in the morning, and the only place that I knew I could write one down and read it all day while at work was on the back of my hand. So, every day I had a new mantra on the back of my hand. It was funny when I would catch some of the other teachers looking at my hand and trying to read it. I would tell them and explain the concept. It got to a point where some of the teachers would find me and ask, "What is it that you are working on today?" We were able to share the lesson together. They would tell me how they struggled, or how they had overcome the lesson I was working on. We would give each other more tips and tricks to fully embody what I was meant to learn that day.

Your mind isn't being "bad" when it says unkind things to you; it just doesn't know any better. By doing affirmations, you are showing your mind the new beliefs that you are ready to take on, so that you can live a better life.

Affirmations can help you send out the energy that you want to have and the energy that you want to attract. It can help shift your energy in any situation. If you go to work saying, "Today is going to be horrible, I don't want to go to work, everyone is mean to me," you set the tone for your day. Work is probably going to be horrible for you, and the people that you come into contact with are probably going to be mean to you. You created it that way.

Even if you have to fake it, don't ever start your day that way. The moment you crawl out of bed and your feet hit that floor say, "Today is going to be a great day."

Reiki wisdom

Reiki is a form of healing that dates back thousands of years. It uses the Universal life force energy as a channel for those who are receiving treatments. Not only is Reiki a wonderful healing tool, but there are five principles that Reiki practitioners use as spiritual guidelines to live by:

Just for today, do not be angry.

Just for today, do not worry.

Just for today, be grateful.

Just for today, work hard.

Just for today, be kind to others.

The International Association of Reiki Professionals (IARP) has reworded these principles.

The modified principles are:

I release angry thoughts and feelings.

I release thoughts of worry.

I'm grateful for my many blessings.

I practice expanding my consciousness.

I'm gentle with all beings including myself.

I recommend that you write these affirmations on a note card and post them near your bed. Make these words the first thing you see when you get up in the morning, and read them before you drift off to sleep at night.

You may be wondering why the IARP reworded the phrases. It is because the brain doesn't understand the word "not." It also doesn't understand the word "can't," just so you know. When the brain sees the phrase, "I will not be angry," it takes out the "not." So instead your brain is actually saying, "I will be angry." That's not the message we want to tell ourselves every day.

For this reason, when you create your own affirmations, you have to be very careful and clear. I have also heard debates on whether or not the brain picks up the word "will," and that is because will implies that it has not happened yet, that it is outside of yourself.

"I am" is actually your best way to phrase your affirmations, even if they aren't fully true yet. "I am" tells your body and your energy that you already have the quality that you are trying to bring forth in your life.

If you know which of your chakras are out of balance, you can use affirmations to help balance or open them.

The root chakra is connected to the *I am*.

The sacral chakra is connected to the *I feel*.

The solar plexus is connected to the *I do*.

The heart chakra is connected to the *I love*.

The throat chakra is connected to the *I speak.*

The third eye chakra is connected to the *I see.*

The crown chakra is connected to the *I know.*

If you think that you have a blocked chakra, then use these tools to create the empowering affirmations that open and align you.

There is a mantra that self-help author Emile Coue made famous: *"Every day in every way, I am getting better and better."* I love that one because it is simple, easy to remember, and can be used in any situation.

Successful people know how important affirmations are. Athletes know that you have to say that you are going to win the race, before you cross the finish line.

Stay in the positive vibes when creating your affirmations, affirm the things that you want to be, do, or have – not the things that you don't.

Jack Canfield came up with an amazing five-step method that I will share with you here:

1. Enter the now.

That one is fairly easy that just means that you use the "I am" instead of the "I will"

2. Stay positive.

This one is telling you to make sure that you say what you do want and not focus on what you don't want. Instead of saying, "I don't want to be alone this year," say: "I am opening up my heart and allowing love to enter my life." "I am always connected to other souls and I allow them to enter my life."

3. Be concise.

Less is more here. Use simple affirmations, ones that are easier to remember and say to yourself. Jack Canfield also suggests making them rhyme as a helpful way to remember them.

4. Include action.

Here he is talking about using the "Ing" when you are creating your affirmations. Such as "I am joyfully drivING my convertible to the bank." would be one I would try to do, or "I am so peaceful as I am walkING on the stage to give my speech. The ing shows action.

5. Include a feeling word.

Canfield explains that the best affirmations have both emotion and content. Content is the outcome that you want, while emotion is how you feel about the outcome. So you could say things like: "I am celebrating how healthy I am, every breath that I take I am becoming more and more healthy."

Affirmations Benefits

Deepak Chopra is an author, an M.D, he is an advocate for alternative medicine, the founder of The Chopra foundation and a leader in the spiritual field. You can go to Chopra.com for some wonderful tools to help you go throughout your journey.

The website offers seven benefits of using affirmations on daily basis and they are:

1. "You become aware of your daily thoughts and words, reducing the risk of letting negative thoughts seep in."

The more we become aware of our thoughts, the more we are able to change them, which in turn helps us change the way we speak to others, and how we treat ourselves and others. If you catch your thoughts before they have time to hang out, you are more likely to let them go and move on from them and less likely to stay stuck in them. Instead you just let them flow on through you.

2. You notice more synchronicities in your life, which serves to encourage and motivate you to keep up the practice."

Have you ever had a conversation with someone and then a few hours later, you have a similar conversation with someone else? You may have said, "That is so weird, I was just talking about that." The more you dive into this work, the more it will happen. It is part of the law of attraction. Your new thoughts are producing this new energy, and this new energy is bringing more of that energy into your life. It's like a big circle. It will just keep coming around the more that you make it a part of your life and it will have no end, it will just keep going. You may affirm: "I am so happy and grateful that I am peacefully driving to the bank in my convertible." Then you talk to a friend who is selling theirs at a steal of a deal. That wasn't a coincidence, that was synchronicity.

3. Daily affirmations not only keep you surrounded by things that you want in your life, but they help bring more blessings and gifts."

Let's say you affirm this: "I am worthy and deserving of all the positive opportunities that the world has to offer me." You are not saying that I will only be happy if I get what I want, when I want it and how I want it. You are saying I am grateful for the blessings and gifts that I have and those that are on their way. You get excited over the blessings that you have and the things that you receive no matter how small or big they are. When you are in that state of being grateful for one thing, and then another thing finds you, you become even more grateful.

4. "A daily practice helps keep the small things in perspective. In this high-speed world you can easily lose sight of how large the small things really are. When healthy you may forget to think of how much you appreciate it. A simple morning affirmation sentence of 'I am so grateful that I am healthy' can go a long way."

I remember when I was a teenager, I was very sick with a stomach condition. After a year of doctors, medications, and more pain than I care to remember, I had to have my gallbladder removed. When I was released from the hospital, a family friend who had been dealing with a brain tumor was staying at the house to ride out the hurricane that was due to hit our other house down in the Keys where he also lived. We were both in the kitchen. He was standing at the counter whipping up a batch of fried chicken for us, as I sat at the counter watching him, still feeling too sick to eat this wonderfully good greasy chicken.

He said something to me that really had hit home: "It's funny, you never know how important your health is until you lose it." This man had more serious health problems than I did. You really can't compare a tumor to a gallbladder. He was right though. I never once had said that I was grateful for my health. I didn't even think to. I am grateful now, but that was a lesson that he taught me. I also say how grateful I am for the health of my family – even though, technically, you aren't supposed to say an affirmation that involves other people.

5. "A recent study shows that optimistic people have healthier hearts, and affirmations help you to stay positive."

Now I don't know the science behind this one, but I do have my own logic to put into this. Those who are optimistic tend to have a more open heart. They have love for themselves, love for others, and a love for life. Love comes from the heart and with that much love going around, I don't see how the heart couldn't be healthier than the heart of someone who hates life, and hates themselves. They let their hearts turn cold, not offering it care.

6. "As you continue this practice, others take note and you begin to help those around you without even trying. This in turn helps you keep focused."

All of us, whether we like it or not, teaching by example. It is one thing to say you are going to change into a better person, and another thing to show how you are becoming a better person every day, in every way. When others see you handle challenges with a smile, a laugh, and a positive attitude, it makes them want to learn what you are doing because they want it for themselves. It's that ripple effect. If you do a good deed for someone, they will do a good deed for someone else, and then that person does it for another person. When you see all of this unfolding right before your very eyes, it makes you realize how true all of this is. It is a form of proof that we humans tend to seek. So it makes you do more affirmations, do more good deeds, and so on.

7. "Daily affirmations help keep you in a state of gratitude."

We have already learned the vital importance of gratitude in all situations and during all times. Sometimes though, it can be difficult to find a reason to be grateful – especially if we are going through a hard time. Doing affirmations on a daily basis helps us not only to get to a place of gratitude, but it also helps us to stay in that state of gratitude.

CHAPTER 8

C is for Conscious Living

C

Consciousness, Conscious living, or mindfulness, is the state of being aware. It means being aware of your thoughts, your surroundings, what you say, your patterns. Living a conscious life means that you are living "on purpose," you pay attention to everything that you say and do. You respond instead of reacting thoughtlessly when dealing with a challenge.

How do you know if you are living consciously? Let's take a look at some questions to help you get more awareness about key areas of your life. Be honest with yourself when you are answering them.

Your Financial Picture

Do you have a savings account? Or do you just live paycheck to paycheck?

Those who have a savings account are thinking ahead, planning and preparing. They put thought into where their money is going. Whereas someone living paycheck to paycheck is probably over-spending and racking up credit card debt. I myself am not very conscious when it comes to credit cards. I don't think of how much I am actually spending. I have learned that I am better at having a certain amount of cash to be able to spend because then every item I grab I think how much does it cost. Does that include taxes? Do I really need it or am I just splurge buying? Same thing with buying fast food. We use our debit cards and buy a round of chalupa boxes for the whole family. We spend about twenty-five dollars. When we get the food, we say, "Wow look at that!" It was pretty cheap compared to some of the other restaurants. But there are no leftovers, and I usually have one kid still hungry. Had I thought it over, I could have made dinner at home, with leftovers, for half the price.

I have also learned that even putting five dollars a week into each member of the family's savings account is a conscious money choice. I don't actually miss the money each week and it's there when something unexpected comes up and we need it. Life happens, your car will break down, a kid will need new shoes, the roof will need fixed. It's unexpected, but you have the ability to handle it, and saving some money for a financial challenge is another useful tool.

Enjoying every bite ....

It's not always easy to be in a conscious state. We are so busy running around in life trying to get stuff done that we often forget that it is an important part of the journey. The first time I started learning about mindfulness I was by taking a CBT (cognitive behavioral therapy) skills course with a nice group of people and great counselors. We got stickers for doing our homework and extra ones when we participated in the activities – just like kids.

One day, as I was walking in carrying my sticker covered-binder, I saw it – the most wonderful way to speak to a woman's heart. A big, round, glossy chocolate cake was sitting in the middle of the table with plates and forks beside it. I smiled, imagining how fast I could make that cake disappear. I sat down next to my friends, who were just as excited.

Our therapist came through the door with her books and a warm smile. She greeted us and then cut the cake into tiny slivers passing them out to each one of us.

"Look at it." She said, "But don't eat it."

What? I asked.

"Just look at it."

Cake is meant for eating, not looking at.

"What do you see?" she asked each one of us.

We had to look at it and only tell facts. For example, you couldn't say that you liked the color of the chocolate. You could only describe.

Then we got to touch it. Again, you couldn't say that you didn't like the feel of the stickiness on your fingers. Just that it felt sticky, or the cake part was spongy.

Next you were able to smell it. I could smell flour and lard.

Finally came the best part after fifteen minutes of drooling over it, we got to eat it. Oh but wait, we couldn't have a big bite. We had to have this tiny, microscopic bite. We had to describe the texture and taste before we could swallow. We had to do that with each bite. That took another fifteen minutes. It was the smallest slice of cake I ever had, and I think I broke a world record of how long it can take to eat cake.

Over the next few weeks, we had to do this with different foods every time we had class. We were also asked to do this at home for our homework. Everything that I put into my mouth took me a long time to eat, so I stopped eating more than I needed. I found out how gross fast food is when you slow down and actually taste it.

Your Body and Exercise

Now ask yourself. Am I overweight? Am I too thin? Is it because you don't stay mindful about what goes into you mouth? I notice on the days that I pay attention to what I eat I make healthier choices. I drink water instead of soda when I am mindful and eat a salad over chips, but I have gained a few pounds by not being mindful, a consequence brought on by myself.

Same thing with exercise. When you are living on purpose, you decide to make the time to exercise, to push through even when it is tough, or you are tired. I know many people that love exercising, who are passionate about it. It is true that you feel better when you exercise, because you produce serotonin in your brain, elevating your mood and your confidence. That doesn't mean it is easy though.

I used to go to a group Zumba class with one of my friends. We were both preschool moms and we would do the class three times a week at a wonderful woman's house with a studio in her garage. It was great fun, and with her support we were able to push ourselves.

Wants and Do's .....

Ask yourself why you do the things that you do?

What is it that you want?

Why do you want it?

Do you want it because society tells you that you need to have certain things in order to be successful or accepted?

How will you feel when you get it?

What action are you taking to get the item or goal that you want?

Why do you work at the job that you do? How does it make you feel?

Why do you surround yourself with the people that you do? Do they fill your bucket up or take from it?

Ask yourself questions the same way a child asks questions in school when they are trying to learn to do something for the first time.

Meditation

Meditation is another part of living life on purpose. Meditation means going within ourselves. It helps us to relax and become more aware. The goal is to quiet the mind.

A woman named Gladys who I refer to as my other mother, was the first one to explain to me that I needed to still my mind when I was about 8 years old.

But I can't I told her, I always have thoughts. I can't stop them.

"Yes, you can." she said "Lay in your bed and just listen to the sound of the fan going. Don't let any other thoughts come in, just lay there still and listen to it." she explained.

I never could do it as a kid. Now I often meditate. Sometimes I sit at the dining room table when the kids are at school and my husband is at work. I am able to stop and just listen to the sounds of the refrigerator. Many people don't even realize that the refrigerator makes noise. You have to stop and sit in the stillness in order to hear it.

There are many enlightened beings who have an easy time going into a still mind. For most of us, meditation isn't that easy. We have to do lists, worries, recipes, archery tournaments, and vet bills etc., going through our heads. The more you practice though, the better you will get at it. Many of us have to do guided meditation in order to discipline our minds. You will find endless meditations on YouTube. You can find specific ones for anything that you might need. If you are having a bad day, find one that helps you release negativity, or balance your chakras, or boost your confidence, or help you with self-love and acceptance. Use them to clear your karma and cut cords of negativity, and release soul contracts with people who no longer serve your highest good. The point is that no matter what you are facing, there is a meditation out there that can help you get through it, release it, and move forward.

Some people say that they don't have time to meditate. Unlike affirmations, you should never try to do a meditation or a hypnosis while driving or operating machinery. You also shouldn't do it in the bathtub, or while the kids are screaming through the house. You will need to sit or lay down comfortably for a certain amount of time. Get up fifteen minutes earlier than usual to give yourself the gift of starting the day off right with a clear and level head.

Everyone, every human that is here on this planet, needs to do some sort of meditation every day. If you can be like one of those monks that take a vow of silence and spend the rest of your days peacefully in a temple somewhere, that is awesome and more powerful to you. For the rest of us though, just take some time out of your day, you won't regret it and anything that you do that day you will have more patience and awareness to handle it all. Meditating doesn't just benefit you, but it benefits the other humans that are a part of our lives.

The days when I meditate before coming out to talk to my kids are days when, even if we're running late, we aren't in a grumpy rush. That energy starts with me. Meditation helps keep me peaceful all day.

Meditation also comes in other forms. In Christianity meditation is praying, it's saying the rosary. It is focusing all of your attention on the God who created you. Buddhists also have different forms of meditation the ones I have found include a chant or mantra. Shamanism also has a bit of a different one that I have noticed. Some of the most powerful ones that I have done add breath work.

There are myths that say that it will take someone years to get any benefit from meditation, but that is not true. The days that you meditate are the days you will see and feel the difference in yourself.

Try it for a week straight everyday, give yourself 15 or even 10 minutes. Find one that you really like and dedicate that time to do it. Journal how you feel after you are done.

If you can't find time in the morning to do meditation then maybe you could find some time before your afternoon nap. If you can write down how you feel before the mediation and then write down how you feel after you finished with the meditation and keep track of it for that week. Can you see the difference?

Vishen Lakhiani, the founder of Mind Valley, which is a website with many resources and classes wrote an insightful book called *The Code of the Extraordinary Mind*. He explains topics such as different levels of consciousness, he shows an amazing meditation that helps you purposely focus on things that we as humans want. For example, he has you think of a loving moment or someone you love, and he guides you to truly feel that love. He shows you that any time you want to feel loved, all you have to do is go into that state of mind, really thinking and feeling that love. By doing the simple mediation that helps you feel the love within and shows you that you can feel that love anytime that you want to, it's always there you just have to quiet your mind long enough to feel it.

There are also a number of meditations out there that when you put the headphones on you get to hear different healing vibrations, different beats and some offer subliminal messaging. Some of my favorite ones have been the ones that have the 3d effect. They aren't very long but they are very powerful. I did one where there was a fire crackling in the distance, I could feel myself walking to the fire. There were Indian men chanting something I didn't understand at a human level (because I don't speak the language) but I knew in my heart what was being chanted. I could feel the vibration of change and the cells of my body igniting. The change was intense but I could feel it working.

Sometimes meditation can happen without you even realizing it. Have you ever caught yourself while lost in a daydream – like the kid sitting in the back of a math class? It feels like being on a completely different planet. You were so focused on the daydream that you jumped when the bell rang and it was time for you to switch classes. Daydreaming is a form of meditation.

Meditation at work...

If Oprah can find time to meditate, then so can you.

I have an Amazon prime membership and with this I am able to listen to a number of free meditations, and affirmations with the app on my phone. Some of the meditations on there are only a couple of minutes. I recommend this app to those who have trouble at work. If you have a stressful job or have to deal with difficult people, then Amazon is a quick, cheap only $9.99 for unlimited for non-prime members to take a few minutes to pull yourself together. You can excuse yourself for a couple of minutes and listen to it in your car or in the bathroom if you have to. Consider this, let's say that you have a coworker that is driving you bananas. You now have lost your focus on your job because you are irritated with your coworker. It's more likely that you'll make a mistake because your mind is still thinking about what happened with your co-worker. Your job performance goes down because your mind is drifting off into other things. If you are really angry, then now you are bottling it up and more likely to yell or treat others poorly because you weren't able to let it go.

Isn't it just better to excuse yourself for even five minutes to get your head back in the game and give your job the best version of yourself? Isn't it better to go get a few minutes of peace than to be upset all day? Isn't it better to just let it go and move forward?

Mothers need this too, especially new moms. Having a baby is one of the most wonderful experiences for a woman. It can also be tiring and stressful. Your thoughts are not on your self care, but on taking care of your baby. It's important for you to care for your baby, but you also need to care for you. The baby will be fine if you lay down and do a fifteen-minute meditation. You will not be considered a bad mom for taking that time for you; it doesn't mean that you love your baby any less because you take some time to recharge your own battery. In fact, it actually makes you a better mom. By caring for yourself you have more to give your child, and your baby gets the best version of you. You can get up, go smile at that sleeping baby or pick that baby up and hold him now, feeling refreshed and rejuvenated. Meditation helps teach us patience, and love. It gives us an opportunity to release our pain. Some meditations make me cry because I fully put myself in them. When I wake up though, all the negative unwanted energy that I had is now gone.

Breathwork

Breathwork is an easy way to meditate and can be done throughout your day. It only takes a few minutes and you already have the tools that you need a part of you to do it and that is just using your breath. What is really interesting to me is the fact that every morning when you woke up and were calm and you took ten deep breaths and then took ten deep breaths when you were faced with a challenge your body would go into calm like when you took those deep breaths as you woke up in the morning. You actually train your brain to be calm even when it wants to go to fight, flight or freeze mode because it is like "Hey I know this breathing, oh I am calm "so now you become calm.

Take-Five Method

When I was taking an online Akashic records reading class, we were instructed to come up with a breathing … that not only could we use but one that we could give our clients so that they can use it and learn to be in a calm, meditative state. The one that I came up with is called the take five method. It is one that I use, share with my clients, kids and the children that I sub for when they are getting rambunctious in the classroom.

It is very simple and even easier to remember. Hold out your hand with all five fingers out. Take five long deep breaths, really expanding your lungs, and getting the fresh air deep down to the lowest parts. Inhale and hold in your breath for five seconds, then breathe out, counting 1….., 2…, 3…., 4…., 5. Now pull in your thumb so you are just holding up four fingers. This helps so that you don't lose count.

Again breath in for 5, hold for five and breath out for five. Do this until you have completed at least five rounds. Try and challenge yourself and see if you can breath in for 7 or 10 the deeper you breath the more calm you will feel. I don't want anyone overdoing it or anything so please be careful to only go as much as you are comfortable with doing.

Keep this breathing pattern, whether it was 5, or 10 or whatever number you felt most comfortable with, and repeat until you no longer have any more fingers up. It is also a really good exercise to teach kids, because they seem to calm down much faster with this method and are able to communicate their feelings in a more constructive way. For any parents out there that can't stand the whining kids and tattle tales, this works wonders!

A lot of times we hear that we should take three deep breaths. For me, 3 deep breaths simply were not enough to calm me down. Maybe it is because for me it takes at least 5 for those 90 seconds of emotional turmoil to get over with. My son needs to take 7 deep breaths and my daughter is one of those who is ok after 3, but we are all different so do what your body needs. Breath work is something that you should try to do a few minutes everyday at least twice a day and one of those times really should be when you are feeling completely calm and at peace to try to train your brain to be at that state more often and to get into that state faster when we are in the middle of a challenge.

CHAPTER 9

T is for Tapping and Other Energy Tools

T

EFT – Emotional Freedom Tapping

I remember the day that I first started CBT classes at the local mental health center. It was my first time being in some sort of group therapy. I wasn't fond of the idea, because sharing my struggles with others felt like airing out my dirty laundry. I was already going through life challenges and now I was going into a lion's den where I was sure I would be judged and shamed because of the struggles I was dealing with.

When I walked into the door and sat down at the table, there was an older woman next to me tapping the side of her face on her temple. I wasn't sure what she was doing. She looked very calm and her breathing was nice and slow. The taps had a certain rhythm or pattern to them. The room soon filled up with others. Most of them knew each other and exchanged greetings.

One lady looked at the older woman and asked, "What are you doing?"

"Tapping." the old woman replied.

"What's tapping?" she asked.

Everyone at the table was now watching and listening.

"Look it up." she said.

"It is a form of healing," she added.

No matter how many times they asked, she wouldn't give us any more information. She just sat there quietly tapping until it was her turn to share.

Of course, the rest of us did the wise thing and asked our therapist about it. She explained that it was similar to acupressure. You focus on different parts of the body and say phrases that allow you to release the negative energy. I thought this was an interesting idea, but I didn't put much more thought into it.

A few years later, when Bernadette Louge entered into my life with her tips and videos on her website, I remember her say, "Even if you have done EFT, you've never done it with me, so we are going to do it together."

The way she said it with such conviction empowered me to book a one on one session with her. At the time, I was very judgmental and self-critical. So when she told me that we were going to be doing a Skype video together, my heart began to race. Something inside of me knew this was going to be life-changing for me, and no matter what, I needed to push through my fears and insecurities in order to get the change I desperately wanted. That was by far one of the best choices I ever made. I opened up to her, telling her my darkest secrets knowing that at this point I had nothing to lose.

We talked, I cried, and we started to tap... I cried more, and we tapped more. All of a sudden, she said that a particular person was an "idiot" for something they had said to me, something that I had allowed to become a belief. I couldn't help but laugh when she told me this. One moment, she was in a peaceful state, with her eyes closed and tapping along with me, and the next moment, her eyes were wide open and looking into mine. She wanted me to know that she meant it. Again, this message went deeper – she was speaking to my soul. After just the first round of tapping, I already felt better. It was amazing how fast my energy had begun to shift and release.

Bernadette explained to me that I was going to have to keep digging into my past and my emotions and tap on them every day. This is one of the fastest ways I have found for healing something. Within moments, you can begin to feel a little relief.

There are different teachers who do EFT in their own way. Some only focus on releasing all the negative energy, while others not only release the negative, but they also add some positive to it by replacing the old with new beliefs.

I don't think that there is a right or wrong way to do EFT. Like anything else, try different approaches to see which one works best for you. What works best for me may not be what works best for you. But I will tell you that EFT has helped everyone I know who has tried it, from adults to children.

EFT has been proven to help with:

1. Stress
2. Anxiety
3. Phobias
4. Depression
5. Sleep (those who use EFT sleep better)
6. Chronic pains
7. Fatigue
8. Those who suffer from PTSD
9. Food cravings and emotional eating
10. Headaches

My personal favorite is how it helps with our emotions.

Most of us have dealt with at least one of those challenges on that list. None of them are any fun, and all of these issues can cause problems in our daily lives. They prevent us from functioning at our best level and giving those who are important in our lives our best self.

EFT can be quick, taking only a couple of minutes to get in a few rounds. Or you can go with your gut and stop when you feel that you are ready. Sometimes that can take twenty to thirty minutes, but it never feels that long.

YouTube Videos for Tapping

The videos by Brad Yates really come in handy. He has a tapping video for most any challenge or emotion that you may be dealing with. I like to listen to him because I know the points well by now. All I have to do is close my eyes and really feel what it is that I am trying to let go of.

Gray Craig also has YouTube videos and conferences where he shows you not only how to do it, but also shows the results other people are getting when he pulls them onto the stage and taps with them. He explains what EFT is very well and he also introduces you to the "Unseen Therapist" – another powerful tool to help in your healing. The "Unseen therapist" is more of an energy in my experience, but I have felt a real difference when I have invited her in and asked for her guidance. Gray Craig also shows you how to find the squishy part on the back of your hand where you can gently tap to just melt the stress away. This is a tapping technique that you can do even when you're around other people.

Japanese Acupressure

The next tool that I would like to share with you is an ancient Japanese instant stress release technique using your hands and fingers. Each one of your fingers is related to different emotions:

1. The Thumb has to do with worry.
2. The pointer finger is related to fear.
3. The middle finger is connected with anger (This one is funny, since when humans get mad, they sometimes hold up this finger at the person who made them angry.)
4. The ring finger is connected to sadness.
5. The pinky is linked to your self-esteem.

This technique is great because you can do it any time, any place, anywhere. It is easy to be discreet.

Here is how it works:

When you get upset, name the emotion, then say, 'I accept the emotion,' and then squeeze the finger linked to the emotion you're feeling for two to three minutes. You should start to feel the pulse in your finger, and when you do, you'll know that you are doing it right. After a few minutes, release the finger. You can do it again if you feel it's necessary.

Some say that it is good to do a round of pressure squeezing on all your fingers every day. They say that it is even more powerful and beneficial if you do both hands, because your fingers are linked to the organs in the body.

When I first learned about this method, it was during the summer when both of my kids were out of school. They had been picking on each other all day. My son who's name is Chance approached me, sobbing about being angry with his sister, but I couldn't understand what he was saying; he was so upset that he was making animal sounds instead of words.

I asked him to at least tell me what he was feeling so I could help him. I asked, What are you feeling right now?

"Anger" he growled.

I grabbed his middle finger and began to squeeze. After a couple minutes I asked him if he was ready to talk.

"Yes" he grumbled. His angry tone matched his face. His eyebrows were Oscar the grouch-like as he glared at his big sister.

Ok. I said.

"Well, he said…" was all that he was able to get out when I let go of his finger.

Instantly, the color of his face went from red back to its light creamy color. His eyebrows went back to their normal resting spot. Even his breath had a peaceful pattern.

He flipped around and looked down at his hand and then back up at me. He didn't say anything for a moment, still trying to figure out what had happened.

I'm listening to you Chance, I said.

"Well I was mad but I'm not now." He said, confused.

He walked off to his bedroom as if nothing had happened. I sat at the table laughing at the power of this stress reliever. To watch my child, who was frustrated and on the verge of a full-blown tantrum, suddenly stop, looking as surprised as me, was a parenting highlight for me.

Reiki

Reiki is another ancient healing technique that the Japanese teach us. Reiki – Rei – means "God's Wisdom" and Ki means "Life force energy". It is done by laying your hands on different parts of the body to allow the life force energy to flow through you to heal you as a whole, or to let the healing energy flow through you to heal another person or animal.

Reiki is not a religion, it is a spiritual science. There is nothing "evil" about it, as some people with religious beliefs may think. It is your own energy, the energy that makes up who you are. It is lovingly, and freely sharing, allowing yourself to become a tool. You surrender yourself to the greater good, the energy flows through you to the intended person, group, animal or situation. Science has proved that we are energy bodies and we have an energy field. Reiki helps that energy flow. I have heard different responses from people when it comes to this idea. The manual that my Sensay uses to teach others explains that Jesus was a Reiki healer. When he laid his hands on people, they were instantly healed. Now Reiki may or may not offer instant healing for the rest of us. Those who practice Reiki are in no way like God. All we can do is allow the spirit of God to work through us, helping the recipient receive the healing energy.

Pope John Paul II (who was my great grandmother Nani's cousin by the way) was being treated by a nun to help with his Parkinson's disease. In 1 Corinthians Chapter 12 of the Bible, you can read about the different gifts given to us by Spirit. It is all the work of God, but the gifts that each one of us receive are different. Some have the gift of wisdom and others are given the gift of healing.

I read a study about how Reiki was used on people staying in the hospital. The researchers treated half of the patients with Reiki as well as modern medicine, and the other half was only treated medically. It was proven that the ones who had Reiki healed faster, had less pain, and had less complications than those who didn't have Reiki treatments. They felt better and had a more optimistic attitude. We all know that attitude is part of what will help us when going through any challenge. So, improving your attitude is another benefit of Reiki.

You can use Reiki for self-healing or you can go to a Reiki Practitioner. Sensay has also given me some healing and in truth I feel it is more powerful when she guides the healing as opposed to me guiding my healing. While I feel the energy when I heal myself and the warmth of my hands, when Sensay guided the energy, I also had visions – which was really cool. When I do my own healing, I have visualizations where I see and feel the energy taking place, but when it is guided by someone else I am able to see visions of things that are offering me more guidance. Seeing animals and numbers is an example of what I saw with Sensay.

I remember the first time that I had Reiki guided by someone else. My Sensay provided me with the treatment. She knows how to do sound vibration healing as well, so she also did a little of that with the singing bowls.

I went to her house and she had me lay down and close my eyes. The moment I did, I was engulfed in a massive, warm bright light-energy field. I saw different images go by and I asked her what they meant. She would talk when I wanted to know about something but never pushed anything. Reiki helps with mental, emotional, and physical healing. In my case, it was mostly emotional healing I needed, although it did get rid of my headache. I needed the emotional more and one of the interesting things with Reiki is that it can't be messed up, the energy will go where it is needed, and it can't be used for anything evil or with evil intentions. When we were finished, I swear I could have floated out to my car. I was in a blissful state for the next few days.

The Magnet

There are many books and videos that can guide you step by step on how to heal yourself with Reiki. One of the tools I recommend that I learned about online is "the magnet."

Here is how this works. Hold your hands over the area of the body that you feel is giving you trouble, and close your eyes. Imagine that your hands are like a magnet, sucking up all the energy that no longer serves you. I like to visualize negative thoughts and emotions being pulled up into my hands, and then I shake my hands to release all the negative energy so it doesn't stay stuck on me. When I see it being pulled out, it looks like black pieces of metal.

Plucking

Another useful Reiki technique, called "Plucking," is where you envision that you have a pair of tweezers. You hold the tweezers in front of your head, or near your forehead, and "pluck" out any negative thoughts that you may be having. After only a few minutes of doing this, you can begin to really feel the yucky spaghetti-noodle black energy being pulled from your head. Last, you will toss the negative energy aside so that it can be transmuted into the white-light energy field and be sent back to you as a form of love.

Some people like to say, "Pluck, Pluck, Pluck," as they pluck away all of the energy. Sometimes I do this myself. For me, what is more important is the intention behind what I am doing.

Donna Eden's Energy Medicine

Donna Eden is one of the teachers of energy medicine that you can find on Mindvalley.com. She offers a free master class on energy healing. If you have ever heard her story, you would know how Energy medicine changed her life. She battled serious chronic health problems, including multiple sclerosis, that she overcame with Energy Medicine, as she calls it.

Spoon Technique

One of the simple tools that she demonstrates in a free online class is how to use a silver spoon and rub the spoon on the bottom of your feet to release some of the stored negative energy in your body.

In addition to free videos that you can watch, Donna Eden also offers live workshop classes and she has written many books. Online you can find some of her handouts that I would recommend you print out and paste on your wall until you have learned the techniques and remember them.

Three Thumps

One of my favorite of Donna's techniques is the "Three Thumps." She shows you the K-27 point below the collar bone, then she has you tap or thump on the thymus, and lastly the spleen. She explains the benefits of that one and a few others, such as the "crown pulling," which is another good one, especially if you are someone who struggles with headaches. They all take only a few minutes and give you multiple health benefits. It's all free tools, why not try it and see if any of those ones work for you.

CHAPTER 10

S is for Senses

S

Senses = Experiences. Every time we are using our senses, the human part of us is the one sending the messages from our experiences to our brains. The senses would not exist if you weren't living here on Earth. The soul doesn't have these "messengers" feeding our brain information. When you die, while your soul will move on in one way or another, the senses stop working immediately, they were only active while the human body was active.

The senses we came here to experience are these:

Sight
Hearing/Sound
Taste
Touch
Smell

When we experience anything, most of the senses are involved. The Senses are also what triggers off most of our memories that we have. For example, maybe you baked chocolate chip cookies with your grandma or mom when you were a child. Chances are that when you walk into a house where the aroma of freshly baked cookies tingles your nose, you'll feel a sense of comfort, taking you back to a joyful memory of feeling safe and loved.

The opposite would be true if every time you smelled fish you instantly felt like throwing up because of the times you were seasick and vomiting over the side of a boat. Or is that just me?

When we create memories there is no doubt that all of our senses are there, because that is how we experience life. In order for you to make positive new beliefs and find new ways of being, I think it's important to bring our senses into the mix. What we want to do is try and bring in all of our senses to offer ourselves healing and comfort.

These exercises won't be hard to do. I have already talked about some of the ways that we can bring in those senses.

Sight

Let's start with sight. Have you ever heard someone say, "Be careful what you see, because once you see something you can never unsee it?" Or maybe you have heard the phrase from the bible about "guarding your heart." Proverbs 4:23-25 "Watch over your heart with all diligence, for from it flow the springs of life. Put away from you a deceitful mouth and put devious speech far from you. Let your eyes look directly ahead and let your gaze be fixed straight in front of you."

Some of the things we see can be very damaging to us. I remember at thirteen years old watching horror movies with my friends who loved horror movies, the scarier the better. One night they decided we were going to watch, *The Exorcist* with Linda Blair. I hated that movie!

I didn't sleep for three nights because of that. Every time I closed my eyes I would see the movie replaying in my head. I knew from conversations with my dad that it's rather easy for a demon to enter your body, especially as a teenager.

Knowing this information about demons brought me a little closer to God those few days. All I did was pray. I didn't want anything evil coming my way. We watched other horror movies that didn't keep me up but did give me nightmares. I am careful now because I learned that lesson. If something too scary, too violent, or too sad comes on the TV, I snuggle close to my husband, close my eyes, and plug my ears.

Sight can be used as tool for your healing. You can go outside and watch for birds, read the pages of your favorite book, watch your children play outside at the park. I like to write on bright colored sticky notes some simple affirmations to help me with a specific situation.

Example when I was having a hard time in my marriage some of the affirmations that I had are: I am willing to SEE this differently, I am willing to SEE this from his perspective, I am open to Seeing new possibilities.

If you haven't already done so, I would encourage you to write down positive affirmations and put them around your house and your workspace. That way it is in sight.

You may want to get some colored light bulbs and sit in a room with one lit for about thirty minutes. Pick a color that is calming for you. For example, emerald green is a very calming color for most people. Green is associated with the heart chakra. Some shades of green match the ocean waters, maybe reminding you of a time when you watched waves gently glide up onto the sand beneath your feet. So a green light would be a wise choice for you. But let's say you had a traumatic Christmas one year as a child because the Christmas tree fell on top of you as you tried to climb it to grab a candy cane. Then seeing green may fill you with fear and would not be a color I would recommend.

If you like to be creative, visual art is another way to develop your sense of sight. You could paint, draw, or do coloring books for adults. It's also a good way to express your feelings and inner seeing.

One of my clients, who is also a friend, found a new hobby after the death of both her parents. She created what she calls, "pour paintings." She would choose colors, whether she realized it or not, based on her mood. Her arm movements also told me how she was feeling. When she would move the canvas slowly, with each turn and twist, beautiful swirls would appear. But if she was frustrated or upset in any way, her movements were faster, and the painting was sloppier and unfocused.

I had the pleasure of learning how to do this from her. She also showed me the blow torch method. This has nothing to do with expressing anger; quite the opposite. When she used the blow torch, she was laughing and happy. (She is an Aries and we do love our fire, so I am sure this played a part in it.) She had figured out that painting helped her handle the grief and the loss she was feeling. The heart shape is a symbol that she associates with her parents; it was always fun to see a heart pop up in anything she created, giving her that extra reassurance that they were still there with her.

The paintings fill my friend's garage, living room, and hallway. I love the paintings in the "remembrance" room she created in honor of her parents. Each one is different and has colors that you can really focus on and fill your body with that healing color that we may need at times.

I would recommend the color yellow to someone who needs to feel warm. Think of it like the sunshine. My sister-in-law is not a fan of yellow; it is safe to say that she hates the color yellow. She even refuses to eat the yellow M& M's. Any song that talks about yellow is on her "Get it off the radio now!" list. For most people, yellow is warm and welcoming. Not for her though. She even feels bad when she buys gifts for any of the kids because she tries to give them each their own color, and when she hands one of them a yellow object, she feels like it shows this child that she cares for them less. We all know that is not the case, but it is something that crosses her mind. While colors can bring on positive emotions for some it can also trigger negative ones. When I dug deeper into my sister in laws negative reaction to the color yellow, we found that it stems from some childhood night terrors. From the ages of 13–16 she would have the same nightmares a few times a month. My sister in law further explained that still to this day she sometimes will have the dreams. So her feelings that she experiences when seeing the color yellow are fear, anger, and sadness.

Personally, I like pink and red. I wear red more these days because it is my husband's favorite color and I can see that it puts a smile on his face. My hair has pink highlights in it so that whenever I see it, it makes me smile. For some, red can feel like an aggressive color; I wouldn't recommend for those people to sit in a room with that color too long. Purple can be a calming color, and so can blue.

Please don't surround yourself with too much black and grey, those are very sad colors. Don't get me wrong, a lot of us love wearing black because it makes us look thinner. However I also have enough other things on like my hair and makeup that make sure I shine brightly. We associate black with pain, loss, and sadness. So surrounding ourselves with too much of it will most likely not be a good thing.

Here is a quick color guide to help you choose a color based on what you need:

Green is the most common and probably the safest of all the colors. It is linked with the prana life force energy that flows through our bodies; it can produce feelings of harmony and can balance our energies.

Yellow is a color of wisdom and energy brought to us by the sun. It can help us clear the fog out of our head and help balance us mentally.

Orange can offer spiritual healing, but orange is also s color that you want to limit your exposure to because it can cause us to feel aggressive or it can sometimes send that message to others.

Red is good for stimulating our aura and can help with healing our kidneys; but just like orange, it is one that you should only expose yourself to for a few minutes; too much of it will also cause aggression and irritability.

Blue (like green) is really good color to help you relax, unwind, and let go. It helps relieve stress and can help you get a better night's sleep. If anyone is suffering from insomnia, I would recommend laying down near a blue light.

Violet is another fantastic color for relaxation. It is also good for opening up psychic centers and enhancing our soul gifts. It simulates the energy to flow through our bodies and can help unblock areas that might be clogged up inside of us due to trapped energy.

Find the color or colors that make you feel good and find creative ways to use them in your life.

Do you want to buy a colored light or candles?

What would you like to create with that special color or colors?

Do you want to wear a shirt in your favorite color?

All of those choices involve using your sense of sight.

What other ways can you use your sense of sight to help you?

Hearing

The sounds that we hear, just like what we see with our eyes, can be both good and bad. Sound can affect and enhance our mood and shift our energy. It can also hit us the wrong way and cause feelings of irritation to come up.

Music

Music helps most of us get through our day. We listen to it in the car, at work, on our phones, and we hear it when we watch movies.

The music that makes one person happy, another person can't stand. It's very personal and subjective. I have friends who believe that the point of listening to sad songs is to help you release your emotions. My friend Ashley was the one who first explained that to me, because I couldn't grasp the idea of wanting to listen to sad music. Personally, I am not a fan of any music that isn't upbeat. She explained that some people need it to help give them a good cry. I can see her point, but some of us super sensitive people have no trouble crying. I don't listen to most country songs for this reason.

I remember visiting my mother-in-law one day when she was having a difficult time. She wasn't feeling good, in a lot of pain, and she was feeling sad. The radio was playing in the background. Every song was so sad. Songs about cheaters, liars, death of a loved ones, and broken hearts. I understand how the world works, that stuff really does exist, I am not denying that bad things happen to people all the time. However, I felt happy before I started hearing all this music. By the time the fifth song rolled around, I was going crazy. It was another broken hearted, sad song. Singing about how they didn't know how they were going to live without the lover they lost.

I said to my mother in law, "Bobbie we have got to turn this off now. I swear, one more song like this and I AM going to slit my wrists in your bathroom and you will have to clean it up!"

If I had walked in feeling happy, but after hearing those songs, I could see why she was struggling with sadness. When we changed the station to some upbeat pop, my energy quickly lifted and my mother-in-law's spirits lifted as well.

One of the things that I would recommend to others is to have different playlists. Have a few songs that are your go-to songs when you are feeling down. Songs that makes you want to dance and smile. One of my go-to songs is "One foot" by Walking on the Moon. It gives you a positive message and has a nice rhythm to it. What are your go-to songs?

Sound Healing

Another way that we can use our sound sense to benefit us is by doing sound healing therapy. My Sensei is a sound healer. She uses singing bowls to create what is called a "sound bath." You lay down and she surrounds you with different singing bowls. She even places some on your body. She uses a mallet to strike the bowl and create the vibrations. Since the body is made of energy, the sound waves produced by the bowls connect with our energy field, healing and moving energy that may be trapped.

Tibetan singing bowls can range from inexpensive ones to a few thousand dollars. Most of the ones I have seen are hand crafted in Nepal. I like to hold the bowl in my hand, feeling the vibrations, and listening to the sounds. It feels almost like taking a deep breath, giving me instant relief.

Solfeggio healing frequencies

Another sound one that I have personally felt the benefits from is the Solfeggio healing frequencies. Solfeggio's are notes with HZ (cycle per second frequency).You can receive these sounds from singing bowls, tuning forks and of course you tube. Power thoughts meditation club has an amazing one that is about one hour long that you listen to with headphones and can still go about your day while listening.

Solfeggio tones have been proven to help with:

1. Lowering your blood pressure
2. Lowering your heart rate
3. It reduces your stress
4. Offers relief from depression

5. Can help you stay focused

At a hospital in Minnesota there was a nun there who is the head of the complementary medicine department. Her name is Sister Ruth Stanley, she got to witness first hand the healing that Solfeggios have on people. The patients at the hospital who listened to the Solfeggios actually had relief from the pain that they were experiencing.

There are six main Solfeggio frequencies:

1. UT -396 HZ

Is used to help you find liberation from fear and guilt and it also helps you turn your pain and grief into joy and happiness.

It cleanses away the negative feelings, the negative beliefs that you have about yourself and other people, it helps you release the ideas that are not of the highest good for you, it helps you uncover any hidden blocks that you may have that are holding you back in your life and it also helps you find freedom from fear.

2. RE 417 HZ

This tone is going to help you make the changes that you want in your life. It produces positive energy to accomplish this change that you seek. It also helps clear out negative or destructive influences brought on by past events. This tone can even cleanse our energy system from traumatic experiences that we have had in the past.

3. MI 528 HZ-

The frequency of 528 is one that I feel is more popular or used more by us humans. It is used in the repair of our DNA putting us back to our original state where we were pure and filled with love. It is also known as the miracle frequency because those who do listen to it frequently experience more miracles, luck and feel more positive. With this tone you can find more clarity of your mind, creativity and inner peace. This one also enhances the life energy that is inside of you. It paves the way to allow intuition to guide you and allows your intention to be one that is for the highest good of all beings.

For me when I started this one, I felt my heart open up more. My chest would tingle as I felt more love for myself, for my family, for others and the world as a whole. I try to keep my frequency at this state or above. One of the Mindvalley.com teachers would say this is "Love or above" and this is the frequency that she is talking about.

4. FA 639 HZ-

The relationship frequency is what I call this one. This one brings with it a harmonious feeling. It helps bring all your relationships back into balance. Where there was friction it helps you find peace with them. A benefit of this one is that when you are looking for help with problems in any of your relationships it puts you into a state of understanding, helps with communication and offers extra gifts of patience and tolerance towards those that we care about in this world. Sometimes it can be difficult to get along with the other humans that are placed in our lives. Our thoughts may go into a negative place which will only manifest into more negativity in our lives by listening to this tone. Our cells go back into the connection that we have with them instead of the annoyance that we sometimes feel for them.

5. SOL 741 HZ-

The solution frequency, this one is the sound of problem solving.

Albert Einstein said that "you will never solve a problem with the same mind that created it". When I listen to this frequency I feel like this is the state that he was talking about when he said that. I associate the ego with the mind that caused the problem (it really is usually the case) and this takes me to that soul level that allows me to find the solution that I am looking for. It opens you up to allow yourself expression to flow from you. When it is listened to on a frequent basis those who do experience a more healthier life, releasing toxins from the body and helping us humans live a more stable life.

6. LA 852 HZ-

The sound of Spiritual Awakening. When I listen to this one I feel my energy lifting up and connecting with Spirit. I feel my crown chakra open and a warm light coming down from above. This one also helps you open up your intuition more. It allows you to live your life at a higher level so you can see beyond the illusions of life. It raises your awareness to know the unseen of this world and the motives that others may have for doing things.

There are three more frequencies that Dr. Leonard Horo-witz found and they are:

1. SI 963 HZ-

This is the sound of oneness. We have talked about that we are all one, one energy and this is what it would sound like. When you listen to it you don't feel so isolated and alone, instead you are gifted the ability to connect back with all of life at its true source and in its purest form. On the days that I listen to this one, I become one with the light. It is considered another awakening tone because it puts us back into who we really are.

2. 285 HZ-

The sound of internal healing. This one Dr. Horowitz found to be beneficial in helping our internal organs heal and return back to their original form. It also helps with our energy field and gives a sense of rejuvenation to the cells of our body.

3. 174 HZ-

The lowest tone that you can go. It is another frequency that offers help to our eternal body and our organs. It encourages our organs to perform at their very best giving them a sense of love and security. This tone is also good to help relieve the body of pain it may be feeling.

Listening to Nature

Another method that you can use is simply sitting outside listening to nature. Some like the sound of the birds as they chirp while flying by, others like the sound of the wind, gently moving the leaves on the tree.

When we lived back in Florida we had many nights where there was a thunderstorm. I used to enjoy sitting outside on our back porch and listening to the rain drops tapping the roof above me, or the thunder as it rumbled around.

The beach offered waves crashing into the rocks.

What sounds help you?

What is something that you can listen to daily?

If you can pair listening to something with your sight sense and you will have an even more powerful healing experience.

Taste

Taste is a sense that we don't always notice when we are experiencing something. But sometimes we can't help but be aware of it – when something you eat is very delicious and your taste buds go into a heavenly state. Or when we're so nervous that we can taste vomit in our mouths (gross but true). When something traumatic happens to us, we usually have that sick taste in our mouth. When we go to the dentist, we may taste blood or Novocain. Later, if you just think about that experience, you can you almost TASTE what it is like to go to the dentist.

I remember when I got my first job at a movie store while living in Florida. I didn't have my license yet, so my mom had to drive me to work. It was my first day on the job and my stomach was tied in knots; my intestines felt like they were turning into pretzels. Then came the taste – the, "Oh crap, I am going to throw up" taste. I said something to my mom about it. She always carries breath mints in her purse. She told me to eat a peppermint to settle my tummy. It worked like a charm. It not only helped my stomach, but also helped calm my nerves. This wasn't the first time that I encountered that fast relief from the taste sense.

When I was in the 7th grade we went on a field trip to Universal Studios Islands of Adventure. It was a hot day; you could fry an egg on the sidewalk kind of day. We waited in line for what seemed like forever. After about two hours we climbed on "The Hulk." It was my first time going on this intimidating roller coaster. As we moved closer to the ride, my heart began to race. Excitement and fear may have the same energy in the body, but my stomach knows what fear is. I was going to back out. I was going to wait at the bottom for my classmates to finish the ride and then I would go on one of the other rides that didn't shoot you out at 70 mph!

My teacher was a great person who understood us kids. He also understood how I worked and how I reacted to things. He had me eat a lifesaver candy, the creamy kind with the swirls on them. It instantly calmed both my tummy and my nerves. Not only did I go on the ride, but I was the first one running to the line to do it all over again.

Tea is another form of using our taste sense to help us. You can find a tea that helps you with almost any kind of health issue. When you sip it, drink it slowly, feel it going down your throat and into your body. If you get loose-leaf tea, drink it with intention and when you are done, you can read your tea leaves to see what your soul wants you to know. Tea can give you a very powerful experience; you can smell the aroma, see the color, taste it; you can feel the cup. If the tea is hot, you can feel the steam on your face. If you want to bring all of your senses into this experience, use a kettle and listen for a moment when the tea is done, as the kettle is whistling, then you can pour the water over your tea bag or leaves.

I don't recommend always turning to food to help us with balancing our emotions and our energy. But I do encourage you to find a something easy that you can use – even if it is just something that you use while you deliberately work on your healing.

What is a way that you can add a sense of taste into your healing practice?

Can you add it to another sense?

Touch

Our next sense is touch. I use touch everywhere I go. If I am at the store I have to touch the stuff around me, when I go to other people's houses I have to touch some of the objects that are around. It may sound weird but it helps me get to know my surroundings, keeps me grounded, and more aware.

Crystals

Crystals are a great way to use our sense of touch and they amplify our energy, you could also add it as part of your sight sense.

There are thousands of gems and crystals that offer multiple benefits in all areas of our life both the physical and spiritual. In a later chapter I will give you some recommendations on some that you can get that help each one of the chakras, so if you want to use them for that too you can. I have a few that are my "go to" during my healing practice.

They are:

1. Amethyst – which is related to the crown chakra and can help relieve you from any headaches that you might experience but my reason why I love it is because it helps during my meditations with my visualizations.

2. Clear Quartz – Quartz are very powerful crystals they produce a high amount of energy. The clear quartz in my opinion is the king of the quartz. It offers intense healing and it also shares that same power to help amplify other crystals that you may be using. It is good for strengthening and repairing your aura, as well as helping the energy flow through you better and releasing you from blockages that you may have built up inside.

3. Citrine – Is also a part of the quartz family and the color can vary from a yellow to brownish red. I love to carry this one on me and not just use it for my healing practice. It helps block negative energy, produces positive energy and helps me keep my mood stable.

4. Aventurine – is a beautiful green crystal that can help you attract more money in your life along with giving you some amazing healing benefits.

It is good at helping balance our emotional energy, helps us clear out old or blocked negative energy and the thoughts of self doubt that we have.

Touch doesn't just have to be a crystal. It can be a stuffed animal that you find comfort in, a blanket or another object that we can hold in our hand. Tapping is another way that you can use for touch. Wearing a chakra balancing bracelet is another good option.

What can you use for your touch sense?

Can you pair it with any other senses?

Smell

The last sense that we will talk about is Smell. We briefly talked about it in the beginning but now I want you to find something that you can purposely put in for this sense.

Aromatherapy & Essential Oils

Aromatherapy has become very popular over the past few years. It can be done by either getting a massage with the essential oils or you can breathe it in (which combines with touch).

Please whatever you do, DO NOT DRINK IT. The oils are not made for us to consume and can have dangerous side effects to the body.

Some people have had mild allergic reactions when it was placed on the skin but other than that it is very safe. Aromatherapy uses the oils which are made from herbs and flowers to help bring about natural healing.

Aromatherapy helps with:

1. Depression
2. Anxiety
3. Stress
4. When applied to skin it can help with joint pain
5. It can help improve your sleep.

Aromatherapy works by activating the parts of the nose that are called smell receptors. These smell receptors send messages through our nervous system and up into the brain. Aromatherapy also helps produce Serotonins which is the "happy feeling" it is the same chemical that antidepressants are meant to produce. But this way you won't experience any of the side effects that modern medicines have.

You can get a chakra bracelet that has the different crystals and gems to help balance each of the different chakras, they also have the lava rocks which you can put a few drops of oil on to wear throughout your day. You can buy a necklace that has the smell coming right up from your neck. A roll on stick at a local health food store is another option, a diffuser is probably my favorite option though because it fills the whole room up with the amazing serotonin making smells. My friend who is a teacher did this to help calm her class down. She would choose an oil and start it while the kids were at lunch. When they came into the room, they calmed down and were able to focus to get their work done. It was amazing to watch, how each one just chilled out, melting into their seats yet still being fully aware of what was being taught.

My son has ADHD and we try to keep a handle on it by using things like diet, herbs and of course oils. He has one oil that he wears when he needs to focus at school and another that he puts on when he struggles to stay calm. He doesn't always like having to put them on, but when he does you can watch him slip into a peaceful state of mind.

My daughter is going through those preteen years (pre-demon training is how I look at it) she didn't like the oils so we bought her the "cheerful balm" I can tell the days that she uses it. In the mornings she is smiling when she is in the car on the way to school. It helps keep her calm because her worry is how she is going to do on a test or if she is going to finish a project.

Incense & Candles

Incense sticks and cones are another good form of using the smell sense, they can be picked up anywhere and are extremely cheap (you can buy them at the dollar store). Incense goes as far back as Egyptian times during the Fifth Dynasty. Like the Babylonians incense was used during their religious rituals. They believed that the incense helped aid them in prayer, just like other religions still use today. Candles are another great option and with them you can also sit there and focus on the flame burning, plus when it is done you can give yourself a candle wax reading and see what your soul wants you to know with that too!

What is your scent for your smell sense?

Can you pull all of the senses together now to form a powerful daily healing ritual?

It doesn't have to take you long, just gather what you want for each sense and use them all at the same time.

Smell something as you are holding something, while listening to something, with a piece of candy in your mouth, while enjoying your special light time and reading those affirmations that remind you of the amazing being that you are. Do this for even 15 minutes to experience a powerful healing that happens with mind, body and soul. Have fun with it, see what works and adjust where you need to.

PART THREE

Energetic Communication from your body, and the Universe

CHAPTER 11

Your Energy Centers (Chakras)

Chakras are energy centers located in our human bodies. We can't see them though (although some can see your energy field and can tell if you have a blocked chakra going on). The Chakras are connected and have a direct influence on your human body. They are linked with our thoughts, beliefs and feelings as well as the organs of the body. Here we will being looking into the roles and benefits that we can have by using your chakras to help you balance out your energies, and release any blockages that you may be experiencing.

The word chakra comes from the Sanskrit word "Wheel". Just like a wheel they are meant to be turning (if they aren't then they are blocked). I see mine as little balls shining bright or little suns. When they are balanced you have inner peace, but if they are unbalanced then you have chaos going on with your energy, your body/health and life in general.

Chakras and yoga are what you would call **energetic BFF's**. By this mean by this that yoga is like a companion and works with energy of your body to keep the chakras happy. Yoga is oftentimes a meditative practice to help the body, mind and soul to be free from suffering and in turn has the mind, body and soul work together to create healing, both mental and physical.

I have heard that there are those who fear yoga because they believe that you are trying to become God. For me it has been yoga connecting me with God and with my soul self creating in me new behaviors and new actions towards others.

Chakras can be found in religions and cultures in India since before Jesus. It is yoga though that we hear more about here in the U.S and not always chakras.

There are a number of benefits that healthy chakras have on the mind, body and soul.

For the mind it helps with:

1. Depression
2. Anxiety
3. Better sleep
4. It can help keep your moods stable
5. It gives you a sense of inner peace.

It helps your body:

1. It helps release toxins in the body
2. It helps with Circulation
3. Strengthens your metabolism
4. Helps the immune system
5. Helps cardiovascular problems

It helps the soul:

1. Creates more positive thinking and less negative thinking.
2. Helps you see and understand your purpose for being here

3. Gives you a clear mind

4. Makes you become more aware and present.

5. Helps you focus.

When your chakras are working at their best you will see life in a new light. You appreciate more and complain less. You are more grateful, loving and accepting of yourself and others. Just like the universal law this will aid you and others because you will have the ripple effect.

In this chapter we are going to put our focus on the 7 major chakras:

1. The **Root** chakra (survival) is the first one we will start with and it is located at the base of your spine. It is linked to being grounded to the Earth, to trusting others and your own sense of safety in the world. It is part of your survival of human needs such as shelter and money.

It is also the one responsible for the "Fight, flight or freeze" response that we humans have.

The color that it is associated with is red which is considered to be the color of life or fire, having a passion, a burning for life itself happens when this chakra is in balance. It is associated with the ages of 0-7 when most of our beliefs are created.

The human sense it is linked with is that of smell.

This chakra is also responsible for our digestion. If you have digestion problems you may want to make sure that your root chakra is cleared of any blockages. It can cause colon problems and constipation too.

The root chakra is where the *I am* comes in. It is what you believe about yourself and the world, the foundations we set for all the other chakras.

Ask yourself these questions:

1. Do I feel safe in this world?
2. Do I trust myself and others?
3. Am I excited about life?
4. Do I have loads of energy or do I frequently feel tired?
5. Do I feel that money is scarce or abundant?
6. Am I fearful?
7. Do I feel supported?
8. Do I have any trauma that was caused between the ages of 0-7?

Depending on what you said then you may be dealing with a blocked root chakra.

I would do Guided meditation while placing a ruby on my pelvic bone, while sipping on some ginger tea would be my recommendation. Also if you are able to stomp your feet when you are upset, will help you feel more grounded.

I am not the best person to talk to about eating a consistent healthy diet. I feel better the days that I eat more healthy but I am human and found joy in some of our human made pro-cessed foods. I am guilty as charged in this area and no, it's not that I don't know how to eat more healthy it is that I choose to eat some of the foods that my taste sense enjoy. That being said I do try to eat the foods that keep my chakras balanced and they are the healthy foods and yes, I do feel better the days that I make wiser choices about what I put into my body.

Root chakra foods that I recommend for balancing are:

1. Beets. I love beets. They are good baked and just add a little bit of salt to them, so yummy. Beets are also good at helping lower your blood pressure.
2. Red apples you know what they say an apple a day keeps the doctor away. It helps unblock the root chakra too!
3. Strawberries everyone loves strawberries.
4. Potatoes especially sweet potatoes

The mudra and mantra that is associated with the root chakra is this:

Mudra – hold your thumb and index finger together so that they touch.

Mantra is Lam. Use a llllllooong L and repeat the sound over and over allowing the vibrations to really move through you.

The yoga pose that goes along with the root chakra is the Mountain pose or downward dog.

Here I also give you the animal or animals that are linked with each one of the chakras because in other cultures they believe that each one of the chakras is connected with an animal. When you know what the animal is you can channel that energy in and you can gain those qualities that the animal is associated with that can help assist you in the challenges that you face.

A symbolic animal for this chakra would be a bull.

The shape it is associated with is the square.

2. The second chakra is the **Sacral** (creativity) located just below your belly button near your hips.

The Sanskrit name translates to *one's own dwelling*.

It is associated with sensuality, sexuality, how adaptable we are to changes, our human pleasures and desires, our relationships and procreation for the earth. It is a place where we tend to trap our emotions or feelings. It is also known to hide our *shadow self*. The things that we don't like about ourselves are hidden in this chakra. The ages that this one is linked with is 7-14 when we are developing our emotions.

The color that is associated with the sacral chakra is Orange.

Our human sense that it is associated with is taste.

It is the chakra in charge of our kidneys, bladder and our reproductive system. If you are suffering from UTI's, kidney stones, or back pain it might be due to the sacral chakra being blocked and it is now manifested into the physical body.

When in balance you will feel more confident and have higher self esteem.

The Sacral chakra is linked with the *I feel* it uses feelings as your guide. The root chakra is where we store our beliefs but the sacral is where our feelings are.

When this chakra isn't balanced properly you may be overly sensitive to what people are saying or doing. In general this one has to do with relationships. If you are struggling in your relationships it may be a clue to a blockage.

Ask yourself these questions:

1. Do I feel anxious?
2. Do I feel confident in myself and my abilities?
3. Do I feel jealous?
4. Do I have a sexual desire?

5. Am I creative?

6. Am I people pleasing?

7. Do I have any trauma that was caused during the ages of 7-14?

Depending on how you answered those questions you may have a blocked sacral chakra. If this is the case then I would recommend:

Placing a gold topaz on your body just below your belly button, with some orange and sandalwood essence oil going in a diffuser while sipping on some cinnamon-vanilla tea.

Foods to eat when trying to balance out the sacral chakra are:

Oranges, carrots, mangos, peaches, orange bell peppers or orange mini sweet peppers.

The mudra and mantra that go along with this chakra are:

Mudra – sitting down in a chair or on the floor, place your hands in your lap with your palms facing up your right palm on top of your left palm.

The Mantra – is VAM and again makes the V VVVVVVV and AAAAAAlonger.

The yoga poses that I like best for this one is The Goddess pose or pigeon pose.

The shape that it is associated with is the crescent moon.

3. The third chakra is the **Solar plexus** (will power) and is associated with our personal power and self control. The solar plexus is interesting because it is responsible for filtering and internalizing the things we are exposed to. It plays a huge role

on our personality and how we perceive things. When we translate it from the Sanskrit word it means *lustrous gem*.

It is associated with the spleen, gallbladder and the liver. It is linked with the ages 14-21 where we are figuring ourselves out, keeping and throwing away beliefs, discovering our identities and also learning who our ego is.

The solar plexus is associated with the color yellow.

Our human sense that it is linked with is sight.

When the solar plexus is working properly we humans have no problem showing and sharing our emotions. When we are happy, happiness shows in the form of smiles and laughter. When we are sad we don't mind allowing the tears to flow and release from our system. If it's not working properly due to a blockage then we may become obsessed with power and the need to control everything. We may be suffering from limiting beliefs, and feelings of shame. When it is balanced you feel confident and empowered.

Ask yourself these questions:

1. Do I sometimes feel powerless?
2. Do I have heartburn?
3. Do I have ulcers?
4. Do I feel good about myself?
5. Do I feel aggressive?
6. Did I have any trauma between the ages of 14-21?

Answer those questions to see if you have a block going on. If you do then I would recommend that you put a citrine crystal above your belly button, while burning lavender oil while drinking Chamomile tea with a splash of fresh squeezed lemon juice.

The Solar plexus chakra says *I do*. So these would be your actions that you do. Whether they are positive or negative depends on the feelings and beliefs that we have.

The Mudra and Mantra that go with the Solar plexus are:

Mudra – Place your hands together between your heart and your stomach. Some people do a praying position but cross their thumbs.

Mantra – is Ram. Again here we also use the long RRRR and AAA when we say it. My husband says that when I say this one my whole body vibrates.

Foods that help with the solar plexus chakra are:

Pineapples, corn, bananas, yellow bell peppers, oats, yellow squash.

If you know that you struggle with the solar plexus then you may be one who benefits from starting your day off right with a smoothie that you blend up with the fruits and vegetables that you need I am not saying you have to add corn into your morning meal but blending up a Banana, mango, strawberry smoothie is sure to help balance out three of your chakras.

The best yoga poses to help balance the solar plexus are the boat pose and the bow pose.

The symbol associated with this one is a triangle.

The animal associated with this chakra is the Ram just like the sound that we make with the Solar plexus.

4. The next chakra we move to is the fourth one and it is the **Heart chakra** (love) and is located right in the middle of the

chest. It is associated with our openness, compassion towards ourselves and others, humanity, tolerance towards others and of course love.

When we translate the word into English from the Sanskrit word it means whole.

It is associated with the color green.

The heart is not so much related to self love as it is to loving others and putting others before yourself.

The human sense that it is linked with is touch.

When the heart chakra is working properly and free from any blockages there is a love, compassion and understanding for all beings. You are truly able to put yourself in another's shoes and feel for them. The love that the heart chakra can produce goes far beyond just our close family and friends but goes out into caring for all humans and all creatures. I personally associate the heart chakra with the mindset of the Buddhists. The care that they have for all beings is admirable at the very least. The heart chakra does offer some self love and acceptance but it's focus is for the highest good of all not just the highest good for thyself.

It is formed between the ages of 21-28 when we grow past that Hallmark puppy love and move into true love. It is where our message center is (from the divine and other souls) and is also the place where giving and receiving happen.

If it is blocked then you may find that you are having some physical problems such as heart problems, upper body problems, difficulty breathing because it is also associated with the lungs.

The feelings linked with this when blocked would be ones of feeling unloved, holding grudges against others, and being lonely.

Ask yourself these questions:

1. Am I holding onto a grudge?
2. Is it easy for me to give and receive things?
3. Do I easily feel loved? Do I find it difficult to love others?
4. Is it easy for you to admit that you did wrong and say sorry?
5. When others have hurt you do you forgive them easily?
6. Do you feel tired more often than not?
7. Did you experience any trauma between the ages of 21-28?

Do you think that you may have a block? If so then I would recommend to you getting both an emerald crystal as well as a rose quartz and placing them on the center of your chest. While burning some jasmine scented incense and sipping on some rose petal tea.

For any of the chakras you visualize them blooming like a flower and releasing any negative energy (black is what I usually see) and then allowing that chakra to be filled with the corresponding color.

The heart chakra to me is the most important one to do that with. I didn't realize when I started all of this how blocked mine really was. I had what the book "*The Emotion code*" calls a heart wall. I listened to some online meditations and constantly opened my heart. I saw it blooming like a beautiful rose and allowed the light and love to fill it up. Whenever I get upset with someone I try as quickly as I can. I move to forgiving them and opening my heart up even when it hurts because I never want it to close again. On the plus side since I have opened my heart more good things than bad happen, I feel more love for others and myself and I make wiser choices because of the compassion I have gained.

It is the *I love* of the energy system. So listing all the things that you love can be another great way to open this chakra and allow yourself to receive more good things because you show a true love and appreciation for what you already have in your life.

The mudra and mantra for the heart chakra are:

Mudra – with your right hand hold your thumb and index finger together and place them near your heart. Do the same thing with your left hand, only place your hand on your knee instead of your heart.

Mantra – is Yam and like all the others is DAAAAAMN to get those high vibes flowing through you.

The foods that help balance the heart chakra are:

Avocados, Kale, Spinach, zucchini, cucumber, green tea, mint, kiwis, green apples, and broccoli among others.

The animal symbol for the heart chakra is that of the antelope.

The shape that it is associated with is the hexagon.

The best yoga poses for the heart chakra are cobra pose and fish pose.

An extra nice healing that I have found that has helped with the Heart chakra is writing love letters. Love letters to others expressing how much I care for them and appreciate them and a love letter to myself every so often gives me that nice extra boost of self love.

5. The next chakra is the **Throat** (expression). Is located at the larynx, it is how we communicate. It is associated with truth, manifesting, inspiration and intelligence.

When we translate the word from it's Sanskirt meaning to English it means *pure*.

The color that most see it is a sky blue although for me it is more of an ocean blue.

The human sense that it is connected with is hearing.

This is an important chakra for us because it is our voice, part of our expression and it is our truth. When it is working properly we are able to communicate what our needs are in a calm manner.

It is associated with the ages of 28-35 and but that doesn't mean that this is when it is developed it just means as we grow we learn to speak wiser, saying things that help and not harm and we really learn to understand that not just sticks and stones hurt, but our words hurt as well. Both others and ourselves. It is important for us to speak kindly, giving words of encouragement and empowerment to all.

For those that may have a blocked throat chakra you may have thyroid problems, you may frequently suffer from sore throats and neck problems. Your shoulders may feel heavy, you may even have swollen glands.

Ask yourself these questions:

1. Do I find it hard to communicate with others?
2. Am I shy?
3. Am I soft spoken?

4. Do I have fears of public speaking?

5. Do others understand what I am saying?

6. Do I gossip about others?

If you found yourself saying yes more than no, you may have a blocked throat chakra. If this is the case one of the first quick fixes that I would recommend to you is gargling with salt water and clearing it up.

Since the throat chakra is our communication and speech I would also recommend that you sing. Go pick a few songs that express how you are feeling at the time if you can't find your own words to get out (yes, even a sad song if that will help you release the energy blocked inside)

Sing loud, even if you can't sing well sing loud anyway letting it completely be free from your body.

Then I would recommend that you meditate with an aquamarine crystal on your throat while burning some eucalyptus oil in your oil diffuser, possibly having a blue light on since blue is related to the throat chakra. Afterwards you could make yourself a cup of peppermint tea.

This Chakra is the *I speak* of the energy system. It is the energy that we send out into the world through our voice and words. It is powerful at all times it is healing or hurting.

When I was volunteering in my friend Ashley's classroom she taught the kids an activity that was with a piece of paper. She explained how the words we use affect others. She had the kids say something that would be hurtful for them to hear and then had them crumble the paper. Then she had them uncrumble it and try to flatten out the paper showing what it would be like if someone said they were sorry. Yes, we forgive but in our hearts there are those wrinkles that stop the paper from ever really being the same, once they are out there we can't take them back. We all have said things that we have later wished we hadn't but the more that we are able to stop ourselves from even letting the words come out the better it is for all involved.

Foods that also help with the throat chakra are:
Honey, Blackberries, Mulberries, and blueberries.

The mudra and mantra for the throat is:
Mudra – have your hands interlaced and facing up, keeping your hands in front of your stomach and have your thumbs touching. Keep your focus on the throat chakra.
Mantra – HAM said hhhhh aaaaaaaa mmmm.
The symbol is a circle.
The animal is a white elephant.

Yoga poses that help with the throat chakra are:
Lions breath and Camel pose.

The sixth chakra is the **Third eye** (intuition) chakra. It is the place where we store wisdom and can unlock our awareness, the third eye has the connection with our own self-knowledge, it is where our imagination exists.

The color that I associate this chakra with is violet blue or a purplish color.
It is located in the middle of our forehead between our eyebrows.

The Sanskrit word is Ajna which means to know or *To perceive*.

It is the power of the Masculine and feminine, the yin and yang and where they meet is right in this chakra.

The sense that this one is connected with is not a human one but what is known as our sixth sense, our intuition.

It brings with it the gifts of clarity and giving you perspective on things that may seem challenging. When we learn to open it this is where we will awaken to the Universe. It is where we will find our answers to life's most difficult questions. It can be our greatest tool for manifesting because it is linked with our imagination.

It is also linked with the different organs that control our human senses, our sinuses and the pituitary gland. It also affects our ears and our eyes. It is linked to the ages of 35-42. It is also the reason we have vivid dreams.

For me one of the ways that I was able to open it easier was by visualizing the colors blue and purple. If it is blocked then you may have problems with forgetfulness or be a selfish person. You may have headaches, nightmares or suffer from hormone imbalances.

Ask yourself these questions:

1. Do I have problems seeing my future?
2. Do I have a hard time using my imagination?
3. Do I have a hard time staying focused?

If you said yes to those then I would recommend that put an amethyst or a blue sapphire on your forehead while burning some lemongrass oil, make a cup of tea that has rosemary in it and I would also say start using Saint John's wort as a daily supplement.

It is the *I see* of the energy that we have in our body. It is seeing what life has for you not in the physical world but where the physical and spiritual worlds meet. It is seeing it in your mind, then creating it in your waking life.

The Mudra and Mantra for the third eye is:

Mudra – hold your hands in front of your breast bone with your two middle fingers standing up and touching and the rest of your fingers are bent and touching at the joints.

Mantra is SHAM – SSSHHHH DAAM.

The animals that are associated with the third eye are:

Hawk and Cats.

The symbol for the third eye is a circle with wings.

Foods that are associated with the third eye are:

Blueberries, eggplants, blackberries, purple cabbage, grape juice or purple grapes.

The yoga poses that are a benefit to the third eye are:

Child's pose and alternate nostril breathing (this one is good to bring both sides of the brain to work together gaining clarity).

I have been very fortunate that I have a very open third eye chakra. My imagination is at times like a child's. I never considered this a bad thing. If anything this is an area where some of my gifts are. A blue or purple light might be another way to open this one up if you find yourself struggling.

The 7th and final chakra that we are going to talk about is the *Crown chakra* (our spiritual connection)

This Chakra is how we achieve true enlightenment, understand and are connected to God and is the place where our spirituality is. It is the Oneness that we all are and it is where we gain our spiritual truth. It is located at the top of the head in the back.

The colors that one may see with this one are white, pink or even gold. I myself sometimes see silver glitter sometimes with this one. The reason why it is these colors is because they represent purity.

The Sanskrit name is Sahasrara which translates into *thousand or infinite.*

The crown chakra is connected to the aura, for that reason this chakra out of all the others has a large focus on detoxifying the body. It is responsible for the whole human energy system, it is where we hold our boundaries and it can be a place where we hold our pain. It is connected to the pineal gland. When working properly you will feel a strong connection with the Source of all creation as well as those that are around us. When I think of this one I see monks (I always see monks with all this spiritual stuff) and I wonder if the ones that have reached Nirvana are living from the crown chakra.

When I work with this chakra on myself I will sometimes feel the top of my head tingle.

It cannot work alone though. The crown chakra does require that all other chakras are balanced and open in order for it to work at it's best.

It is associated with the ages of 42-49 (I wonder if this is because after the age of 40 is when men reach their full maturity?). It gives us our sense of purpose on a soul level.

When it is not in balance you may feel depressed, disconnected from the world, you may be isolated or feel like being a hermit in your own home and avoid the outside world along with interactions with others. You may feel distant from God and lost.

Ask yourself these questions:

1. Do I feel whole and complete just as I am?
2. Do I feel like I have a purpose here on Earth?
3. Do I feel a connection to the Divine?
4. Do I feel abundant?

If you said no to most of those then you may have a block going on with the crown chakra. In this case I would recommend that you meditate with an amethyst or a diamond on the top of your head. While burning some Jasmine incense and sipping some rose tea.

Massaging the top of your head is another good way to stimulate the opening of the crown chakra.

Meditation and yoga are great ways to connect the mind, body and soul and of course the crown chakra.

The energy of the crown chakra is *I understand* it is knowing why we are here, what we were created for and who we were created from.

The herbs that help balance the crown chakra are:
Lavender and sage.

The mudra and mantra are:

Mudra – you put your hands together in front of you lacing your fingers together and keep holding your pinky fingers up.

Mantra – OOOOMMMM.

The animals that are linked with the crown chakra are:

The butterfly because of transformation and rebirth.

And the owl because it represents wisdom.

I love the symbol for the crown chakra it is a lotus blossom. Which is the symbol of rebirth and enlightenment.

The yoga poses that are linked to the crown are:

The rabbit pose and the revolved bound half moon pose.

CHAPTER 12

The Moon Phases and You

"For anyone who knows me, should learn to know me again; for I am like the moon, you will see me everyday with a new face."

—Rumi

For anyone who has looked into astrology, you will find how the planets, the moon and the sun affect our whole lives, why we do the things that we do, the challenges that we need to work through, the gifts we have to offer etc.

The moon's gravity is responsible for more than 50% of the ocean's tidal energy. If the human body is 60% water, does it not make sense that the moon phases affect us humans too?

It was my Sensay who introduced to me the importance of the moon phases. When I was taking Reiki with her, she brought up the moon phases to help with our inner growth. It immediately clicked in my head how much sense this made, and I learned how to use the moon to help me grow spiritually.

We may hear how the moon affects fishermen and farmers. Fishermen believe that "the bigger the tide the bigger the fish." Full moons and New moons cause the fish to be more active. Both high and low tides are caused because of the gravitational force from our moon. Farmers like The Farmers Almanac use a form of agricultural astrology to follow the phases of the moon for planting and harvesting. Which phase is more fertile and which is more dry.

By learning about the phases of the moon and how they affects us as humans, we can learn to use this energy to help us grow.

The moon is considered to be feminine and has a direct effect on our emotions.

Remember this: emotion = mood.

Each moon phase has different cosmic meanings, different vibrational energies, and different emotions that are going to come up for us.

1. The New moon (Beginning again)

When we look into the sky to see what the moon looks like during this time it will be dark to us.

This is the time in our spiritual journey we go into retreat to prepare for a fresh start and the month with a clean canvas waiting for us to paint it. We may feel like being a hermit and hiding out in our own house, not really wanting to speak with others, just getting lost in our head.

It is ok during this time to turn inwards, use this time to release what no longer serves you when it comes to your thoughts. If it doesn't empower you, don't follow it.

Maybe clean out your closet, and with the clothes that no longer fit or that just stay there gathering dust, decide to "let them go." As you place each one in a bag visualize that it is a thought that you no longer wish to carry with you. While you put the clothes in the bag feel yourself letting it go now. When you are finished, take this bag and donate to a local shelter. That way you have the ripple effect. By letting go you help yourself and someone else, maybe even multiple people. It puts out good karma for the highest good of all.

Keep your mood focused on letting go, not on what you think you are losing. In order to allow new people to come, you have to make room for them.

For women this may be the time when you have your menstrual cycle. During a new moon you may have lower energy, feeling more tired to do some of the normal daily tasks. Your libido may also be down. If you get your hair cut during this time it is more likely to grow faster and stronger. Not a good time to start any new projects.

2. The Waxing Crescent (Setting Intentions/ goals)

My son calls this part of the moon God's thumb nail. I think he got it off of "Angel's in the Outfield" because when he was little I loved the movie and the messages it taught, so I watched it and hence so did everyone else.

In our soul journey this is a time of setting those big goals, for hoping in the manifestation of those big dreams and for making wishes on every star. We went into hiding with the last phase, letting go of what we needed to and recharging our battery because we aren't the energizer bunny we can't just keep going and going.

This is the time where we are planting our seeds in our garden.

Power thoughts meditation club says an affirmation that has stuck in my head and comes out during this time:

"Thoughts are like seeds, you can grow flowers, or you can grow weeds."

Same thing with setting up our goals if you focus on the negative then you are going to grow weeds, but if you focus on the positive then you can grow opportunities.

What I do with this one is say a prayer asking God to help me to achieve the highest good for all beings, then I write on a piece of paper "I am so happy and grateful now that ....." Then I put my goals down while holding one of the crystals that I feel drawn to. Next, I fold up the paper and put the paper as well as the crystal into one of my singing bowls. I close my eyes as the bowl sings even louder than normal because of the crystal inside. I feel the energy vibrations of the bowl connecting with the Creator of our Universe then of course I burn it (fire) and flush it (water).

Another tool that I use, I learned from Jim Carrey. Before he was famous he wrote himself a check and then he kept it in his wallet knowing that it was going to happen. I have a check in my wallet and am waiting for it to be the same amount in the bank account.

3. The first quarter moon (action)

This one we see when the moon is a quarter of the way through it's monthly cycle. For our soul journey this is a time where we see many challenges come up. It is the first roadblocks that we face. Be mindful of the choices that you make during this time, some decisions may need to be made very quickly. Make sure all your choices are lined up to bring you closer to your goals, not away from them. You have already had your time of rest, your time of planning, now is the time to make your moves on what you really want. Flexibility is going to be a quality that you are going to have to make friends with right now. You asked the Universe to give you what you need to achieve these goals. In order to succeed you are going to have to stay calm and keep moving forward. The challenges are just helping you grow in order to help you prepare yourself for the new that is going to enter your life. Some of these challenges may be emotions that you need to learn, or stresses that could be common for a person that is going for the kind of goal that you are going for.

During this time a daily to do list is very beneficial. It will help you keep your thoughts on the daily goals no matter what obstacles you may face and when you see the goals accomplished you will gain confidence only amplifying your energy to achieve the next goal on your list. If you have trouble processing some of the challenges I encourage you to write it on paper something like this:

Even though I face this challenge I still choose to accept what is going on or Even though I am faced with this challenge I still choose to go after my goals.

I am choosing to release any stress this is causing me.

Or come up with some of your own, the point is not hanging on to the energy.

You don't want to emotionally charge the events that are going on around you, the more energy you put into them, the stronger the emotions will become and you are more likely to have negative experiences.

Instead write it out, journal it and if you are like me you burn it in the fireplace and allow it to go back up into the Universe where it will transform into love.

If you have ever played any kind of racing game on your phone or computer you know that when obstacles come out in front of you, you don't pull over and wait for the others to pass you. Instead you *reroute*.

I myself enjoy the game on my phone *"Minion Rush*. For me the longer I ran the more concentration and focus I had because as you play, the more points you get the faster your minion moves. But the obstacles still come up unexpectedly and you have to be ready to dodge them in order to move to the next level. You learn to turn in a different way, or jump through a hoop but you don't give up, you just keep moving forward. Like what we are supposed to do in life. We aren't meant to stop when we are faced with challenges we are meant to find out if we stay on this path, or jump to the next.

4. The Waxing Gibbous Moon (Pull weeds, refine or realign)

This is the last phase of the moon before it is full. This phase teaches us that even when we plan things, the Universe has its own plans. It is like there are multiple paths in front of us during this time.

The Waxing Gibbous encourages us to really look at what we are doing and ask ourselves is there a sacrifice that I am going to have to make here in order to move forward with my goals?

Am I willing to make this sacrifice?

Who does it affect?

If I am not willing to sacrifice, do I need to change my path?

The feelings that we get from things changing even when it is a positive change are ones that aren't always comfortable. We may feel anxious or that something isn't quite right. The reason why is even when we are unhappy in a current situation, it is still a situation that we know. We know the patterns, routines and possible problems. It is easier to stay in what we know then it is to go out into the unknown.

Think of this like snorkeling in the ocean. When you are sitting on the boat you are comfortable and safe. You can see for miles and know all your options until you look down. You don't know how deep the water is, or what lies beneath. You have heard stories about people swimming in the ocean with sharks and you have also heard the stories of the people swimming in the ocean with dolphins and fish. One is scary and makes you have anxiety and the other is adventurous and you have excitement. Guess what though, your body can't tell energy wise if it is anxiety or excitement. So jump in the water and swim. What do you have to lose?

Either sacrifice the problems or sacrifice the mission but with this moon I guarantee you the only way is through sacrificing in one form or the other. Each path will lead you to a different result, you must choose which result it is that you want and keep swimming.

5. The Full Moon (Harvesting our garden)

The Full moon can be an emotionally trying time for many people. It has been proven that crime rates are up, that there are more births during a full moon, accidents and injuries. People are more prone to violence and negative thinking.

The sun and moon during this time are on opposite sides which makes us have an internal battle of opposites going on inside of us. The zodiac signs are at opposites so they are also opposite inside of you. You must learn to recognize the two signs that are going on for you. You may feel more moody during this time. Going from loving your partner to wanting to throw them out of the house the next moment. What would normally be simple disagreements are more likely to be blown up into something bigger, anxiety can come for no apparent reason.

During the full moon think of that old Indian chief who told his grandson that he has two wolves fighting inside of him, a good one and a bad one. The one who wins, is the one that he feeds. Feed the positive, pick the flowers and don't focus on the weeds. See what benefits you have gained even if you have to look harder to find them.

Are new opportunities coming your way even if it's not in the form that you expected?

Are you open and allowed to let the Universe give you what you asked for?

Are you allowing yourself to receive from others?

During this time you may feel more creativity and I encourage you to find a way to express that. If your intuition is trying to speak with you listen to it during this time especially. It may take you longer to fall asleep, so if possible allow yourself to take a 20-30 minute nap during the day.

Full moons are a good time for conducting business (listen to that intuition). Try to avoid the shopping because there is a likelihood to overspend right now.

It would be good for you and your crystals to go outside and take a *moon bath* just sit and soak up the light and energy of the moon, your crystals can recharge at this time with you. If you put water in a mason jar with a lid you can drink it the next day and have that energy going into your body (make sure that you have an intention with it so say something like *With this moon charged water I am allowing my body and mind to heal from it's help*).

6. Waning Gibbous (Grateful)

This is when the moon is less big and bright it is coming closer to the last quarter moon phase.

It is a time where it is easier to stay in the positive. You may be feeling that your hard work has paid off or at least now is showing you some of the benefits. You may feel more loving towards yourself, others and the world as a whole, treating people in kind and thoughtful ways. It is possible to show this appreciation in the form of splurging on your loved ones, try to be mindful so that way you don't spend too much. Showing them love though after the emotions of the full moon is a great idea.

It is a time of abundance where you feel good about yourself and about the things that you have been creating over the past month. It is a time when you want to find as much gratitude as you can, in all things. For the goals that you have completed, for where you are at so far on your journey and grateful for the opportunities that are coming to you.

The Universe loves when we are grateful. Write everyday during this time what you are grateful for and why! Put thought into it, put feeling into it, and most importantly put sincerity into it.

Again this is one that I write why I am so grateful and then I put it in my little singing bowl and set the paper on fire before flushing it down my toilet. Find the positive in all things, this is the time where enthusiasm can come very easily to someone if they are willing to be open and excited about even the tiniest details of their goals being manifested.

Tell others that you are grateful for them, do acts of kindness, make a special meal for a friend, give back and be of service to others. Volunteer to make someone's load a little lighter.

If you have watched the secret you know about the grateful rock that the man found and put into his pocket and every time his hand touched it he named something that he was grateful for. You can do this too. With a rock that you find outside of your house in your physical garden, you can find a rock at the river when you are out in nature, you can even use one of the crystals or gems that you use for your healing practices.

If it is winter, light a fire to stay warm and throw in papers saying everything that you are grateful for. You can even sit next to a window inside of your house and just watch the moon, soaking up its energy.

7. Last quarter moon phase (releasing)

This is the time now where the moon is at a quarter again after the full moon we start heading back into the new moon.

On our soul journey this is a time of more releasing, releasing everything that we picked up this month that doesn't serve us in optimal ways. It is a time where you see that even though you may have fallen down you have to forgive those who pushed you. It is letting go of the past, the anger, and grudges. The last quarter moon is another time where cleaning out our closest, our homes, cars and the thoughts and emotions that are inside of us is encouraged, that way you can prepare for the next new moon and the new goals that you want to go after. It is a time to check and see who we have allowed into our life and if they are still meant to be apart of your journey, to check your soul contracts with others and see if they have been fulfilled or if there is more that is needed to be learned.

Forgiveness is probably the most important thing to work on though.

Get a piece of paper, draw a line down the middle and write every crappy thing that happened to you this past month, every mistake you made, every time you were angry just write it on one side. Every mean thing someone else said or did. On the other side next to each challenge write *I am choosing to forgive them, I am choosing to release this energy that I am carrying in me, I am letting it go now deeply and completely.*

That includes you though next to everything you did, no matter how horrible it was to someone still write *I am choosing to forgive myself now.*

Take a shower and as you scrub visualize all the old dense energy going down the drain and out of your energy field. If you need to cry to let go of some of the challenges that you have gone through then go ahead and cry knowing that with each tear that you shed, you are expressing that energy that got trapped in the body and are now consciously choosing to release it, to just let it go and move forward. Listen to a meditation on forgiveness and letting go. Find whatever way helps you peace and release.

8. Waning Crescent Moon Phase (surrender)

There is not much left of the moon at this time, it is now at the very last phase of the moon cycle. Soon it will be gone and we will start another cycle with the beginning of the New moon.

For our soul this is a time where we are resting. We are allowing our bodies and minds to give up control on what we think is supposed to happen and accepting that destiny is a player in this game of life as well.

We watched things enter in and out of our life. We chose to bring in things the same way that we chose to release things. It has all been a cycle of birth and death. Giving and receiving, loving and forgiving and now it is time for us to do nothing but let go. Some say this is the perfect time to *Let go and let God.*

It is time to stop, take a deep breath and just trust that all will work out the way that it is supposed to, even if it isn't the way that we want.

Eclipses have an effect on us as well. There is debate on how long the energy and emotions that we have from them will last. Some say that it will start a couple weeks before, others say six weeks before. It will also affect us afterwards as well having an impact on us for up to six months. During times where we are close to or just had any form of an eclipse it is best not to make any major decisions because during this time our emotions can be all over the place.

Did you know that pregnant women are advised to stay indoors during an eclipse? The reason why is since the body is made up of water and the unborn baby is surrounded by all that amniotic fluid it can actually put you into labor.

Similar to the full moon a Lunar eclipse will have an impact on our sleep which will only amplify the emotions that we are having, causing us to come across as moody.

This can also be used for the highest good though too. During this time we are more connected to mind, body and soul so it can open the door to digging deeper into ourselves and the feelings that we may be having so that way we can purge our bodies of what no longer serves us. When you release and get through the pain, you will experience healing, a form of rebirth. Letting your old self go and the new you to come through.

While a lunar eclipse is more about letting go, a Solar eclipse is about new beginnings. With it you are manifesting so be sure to focus on what you want and not what you don't want.

During this time you may feel restless. You may feel off and not sure why. Some use this time to break down the walls that they have had up so that way they can have a fresh start. Our human bodies will feel more tired and like the moon we will be more emotional.

Many people like to take this time to meditate because the vibrations from the eclipse impact our pineal gland which is linked with our third eye chakra.

Depending on the culture you will hear mixed things when it comes to the solar eclipse. Some see it as a good omen, a positive experience because it allows our minds and bodies to heal from the emotional baggage that we carry.

Others see it as a bad omen believing that we are only deepening our wounds, adding salt to them and causing us more problems.

I chose to believe that it is healing, even when things come up that I don't like it is better for me to take it as an opportunity to heal and grow then to take it as a time to wallow in self pity. Which I have also done but have learned the hard way that nothing good ever comes from this kind of mindset.

CHAPTER 13

Signs from the Divine

When we pray or meditate, we often find ourselves asking for guidance, for help and for some way of knowing the right thing to do. Not all of us can hear our Creator. Some of us can feel him/her some see him/her. The ones who don't have that strong connection with Source though can oftentimes feel lost. It can be a very lonely feeling. But we don't have to feel that way. There are other ways of Source getting our attention and there are even ways that we get an answer almost immediately.

Like anything this Cosmic energy connection can be used for good or for evil. I know some religions believe that some of this is dangerous, but so is a gun in the wrong hands. Does that make ALL guns bad? No! For someone like me, a gun in the right hands means that my family and I will have dinner for the rest of the year. My dad is a hunter and because of him, we get a freezer full of elk every year. I don't have to worry about whether there is going to be a recall on ground beef, because my dad has supplied the ground meat we use. I know where it came from and how it was processed.

Angel cards

Angel cards fall into this category. No, I don't recommend any of the ones that have the devil or demons. I don't recommend the ones that spread doom and gloom and fill you with fear over what is to come. I actually recommend that you stay as far away from those as possible. I do however recommend the ones that are filled with love and light and here is why.

When I close my eyes as I am holding my angel cards in my hands, I ground myself to the Earth below my feet. Then I open my crown chakra allowing my little soul light to go up into the Universe connecting to either the energy of it all which to me looks like the northern lights or if I am in need of a human figure I see Albus Dumbledore from Harry Potter.

My heart is open and I just talk to him, telling my feelings and then asking him for his help and guidance. I also explain that no matter what He tells me even if I don't like it, if it is His will I shall do as He asks. When he looks at me above those half moon glasses he says "So you want my guidance?" The moment that I say Yes, is when a card flies out at me or sometimes a few cards because there is more than one message. The answers are always loving ones because those were the cards that I chose. If you don't feel comfortable with that then maybe buy the positive affirmations with the intention of *what does my mantra, or quote of the day need to be?* The Universe will give you a message and it will help you throughout your day.

A lot of times when I do the cards for myself or others I just ask *What does my soul most want me to know? What do you want me to know?* and I usually get a few cards for that.

The Creator is not human, you will not be able to just call Source on the phone and talk the way that you and I could but you can still connect with Source.

Before I move on to the next few ones I want to share something else with you first.

Carl Jung was a psychologist who said that synchronicities are "meaningful coincidences."

A coincidence according to Wikipedia is "a remarkable concurrence of events or circumstances without apparent casual connection."

In other words, if you are out to lunch talking to your friend about wanting to write a book but needing to take a class so that way you can enhance your skills. Then when you are finished with lunch and you start driving back to work and you hear about the local college offering a creative writing class. That is not a coincidence. That is the Universe trying to get your attention and offer you the guidance to the path that is available to you if you chose to take it.

When you ask the Universe for help be open to how you may get the answer. It can come in many forms and it is up to you to find out what ways work for you so that you can develop that connection and feel that guidance that has always been available to you. Source has always talked to you, it's just a matter of have you been open to the answers that Source is giving you.

Angel numbers

Angel numbers are energy vibrations and messages from the Universe. Angels are said to be God's messengers. One of the ways that they like to communicate with us is through numbers.

You can be going about your day and keep seeing a certain number every time you look at a clock, your phone, or your computer and that is a way that the Universe is trying to get your attention because it has something to tell you.

I like to play the license plate game with the Universe. When I am driving after I say my prayers, I will think of something that is really bugging me and that I am wanting an answer to.

Next I state my question in the form of a Yes or No answer.

Is it in the highest good of all beings for me to finish writing my book? Is this the best path for me to take?

Then I think of two numbers like today 4-Yes 9-No after that I start looking at the numbers around, the ones on cars, at the gas stations even the time on my clock. It's funny because sometimes when that happens I will see one number a few times and then the other number (or answer) and then I question myself *Oh no did I just make that up? What if it is still not the right answer.* It is usually about that time then that I see the original answer in a double or triple digit and then I also end up with a text message on my phone showing me the answer.

If the Universe is trying to get your attention and you are wondering about some of the numbers and meanings I will give you a quick reference but like anything go discover for yourself what each of these numbers mean for you.

When you see the number pay attention to what you were just thinking, usually when the numbers pop out at you it is not because of what is going on right then, it is about what you were thinking about right then.

1's represent new beginnings, creating, attainment, fulfillment, manifesting and being aware of your thoughts. Have a positive attitude, have faith in the Universe. It can be a message that what you are thinking you are creating so make sure you are creating out of love and not fear. Some see this on their spiritual journey quite often. *Ask yourself: Is what I am thinking what I'm thinking something that I want to bring into my life? What outcome do I want? What positive thoughts can I create right now?*

2's Harmony, balance, love, cooperation, peace, courage, partnerships and relationships. When you see the number two it could be a message for you to show more compassion. It is asking you to have trust and belief. Or it could be asking you if you are being trustworthy. Are you compromising and being cooperative or are you being argumentative and insensitive? The number two asks you to show love even when it is difficult or you think the person is undeserving of it. If you are seeing *2's ask yourself: Am I being a trustworthy person? What can I do to live in alignment with my morals and values?*

3's are kindness, joy, imagination, growth, it is the trinity and also the mind, body and soul, Inner guidance, support from the Universe and could also mean adventure to come or an adventure is needed. The Universe is telling you that it is here and ready to co-create your life with you. It is trying to show you your true potential and that it is here ready to step in on your behalf. *Are you using your imagination in positive and productive ways? Are you doing your daily activities with joy? Are you treating yourself and others with kindness?*

4's patience, loyalty, trust, organization, endurance, dependability, discipline.

When you see the number four it could be telling you to have patience with something or with someone, it could be telling you how loyal someone is or reminding you of your loyalties, it may be telling you that it is safe to trust someone, or reminding you to trust yourself. If there is a project that you were thinking about then it may be telling you to get organized or that organization is needed. It is also wanting you to go for your goals, be persistent and not give up. Take action and put in the work that is needed in order to achieve them. The number 4 is a very powerful number and not one that you should ignore. *Ask yourself am I being patient? Am I going for my goals?*

5's are here to tell you that positive change is coming your way. It also means that changes in general are coming and that you should try and prepare. Make sure that you keep focused on the positive. It is here telling you that you are both a Soul and a human body. Balance and health are other possible meanings with this one. It could be the Universe asking you to improve your health. Other possible meanings are life lessons, slowing down and opportunities. *Ask yourself, am I being responsible? Am I being thoughtful of others? Am I ready for change? Do I allow change? Am I caring for my soul and human needs?*

6's are oftentimes called the motherhood number. It is a number that embodies all of the qualities that a mother has /does. Protective, healing, family, selfless, nurturing, service to others, problem solving, responsibility and sacrifices. When you see it, it could be telling you that new things are going to be showing up in the area of family or home. Maybe you will have a new addition to the family, or buy a new home, maybe you will get a new pet. It reminds you to not just worry about money that the money will come, to not give up and keep pushing forward even in the most difficult situations. To always expect good things when it comes to your home and family life. *Ask yourself, am I supporting the people who I love and care about? Am I willing to be selfless or am I being selfish? Are my actions healing others or hurting them? Is there someone in my life who needs more nurturing? Is there a problem that I need to solve? Do I sacrifice things for the highest good of all or do I only expect others to sacrifice for me?*

7's tell you that you will overcome any obstacles that you are worried about. It means being thoughtful of others in your actions, promoting peace and natural healing abilities. It can be a message that good fortune is on it's way. The Universe may be asking you to have determination, to learn new skills to help you overcome those obstacles and to help others. Another meaning is the Universe is giving you a pat on the back, saying good job that it is happy with the choices that you have been making in your life. If you wonder if you are on the right path, wonder no more the Universe has just answered you saying that you are. It asks you to remember your soul purpose and mission here and to keep learning and keep growing. *Ask yourself what new skill can I learn to help me move forward towards my goals?*

8's are always nice to see as they usually bring with them material abundance and career success. It may be asking you to balance the spiritual and materialistic parts of you. It may be an indication that you have a block in your energy system (human body) and could be asking you to align yourself with the energy of abundance. To be open to receive, or a message that you are very close to your goals. It could be telling you to have more self confidence and put in the work to co-create.

On the other side of this number though is that it is a Karmic number reminding you that your actions will always have consequences either good or bad. It is asking you to release any negative thoughts that you have been having and to be grateful for what you already have. When you see this number *ask yourself:*

Am I being fair to all involved? How are my actions going to affect others? Am I being greedy in any way with what I am doing? What choice can I make here that is for the highest good of all beings?

9's are another Karmic number and also have a connection with the laws of the Universe. It can be a message that you are a light worker and need to use those gifts to help others, soul awakening, leading others by your positive example, romance, destiny, service to humanity or your community. It could be a message to have faith or to feel love. It could be asking you to have empathy and compassion for others, to listen to your intuition, to forgive those who you feel wronged you and to be sensitive towards others feelings even when they don't match with your own. *When you see this number the Universe may be asking you what is your passion? Are you sharing your gifts, talents and abilities with others? Does someone need your love or help?* Another meaning that can be associated with this number is that it is also sometimes the number of completion and endings. 9 is strongly connected to our human lessons that we are here on this journey to learn. To be the light in the world even when others are in darkness.

0's always amplify the other numbers that they are with. Alone they can mean a soul journey, a new phase that you are entering in your life, oneness with all of the Universe, your higher self. It is considered to be the God number because it has no beginning and no end. When you see it, it may be the Universe telling you that you are not alone, that you are fully supported and that you put more effort into your prayers and meditations.

If you see pairs of numbers you might be getting two messages so it is a good idea to look into what each one means to figure out what the Universe is trying to tell you.

Spirit Animals

The next kind of signs that we will discuss are spirit animals. We all have power animals, totems and messengers to help offer guidance along our human journey. Spirit animals share information with us to help us balance and grow. When we come across animals think of the qualities that they have, how they function in the world and see what it is that the Universe is trying to tell you through them. Animals don't always have to show up in a physical form for them to deliver a message to you. They may appear in dreams, you might see an advertisement with an animal that stands out to you, you might even just have a feeling or a thought about an animal. Sometimes they arrive because of the thoughts that we are having and they are trying to give you guidance that way, but a lot of times they are showing up for the bigger challenges that you may be facing. Think of your favorite animal as a child. Did you ever question why you were so drawn to it? It is because that animal was there to help you through your life challenges, it may stay your whole life or leave when you no longer need it's help. Some come just to give you messages where others will stay until a completion of a lesson, some will come and go at different times but all have something to teach us.

Totem Animals

My favorite animal has always been the giraffe. For as long as I can remember I have been fascinated by them. I always thought it was because they were so tall and I am very short. I loved the different spots on their bodies and just admired how graceful they walked around.

One of the greatest times for me was when my dad took me to *The Animal Kingdom* and we were able to stay at this hotel where they were right outside our window. Another time was when my husband took me to the Zoo in Colorado Springs and I was able to hand feed them. I had already been studying the messages from our animal friends for well over a year, telling everyone what theirs meant but, I hadn't looked into my own. I just didn't think of it. I knew that one of my spirit animals was a white Siberian tiger but, I found that out in a guided meditation. I was sitting in my living room one day staring at the beautiful giraffe statues that my parents got me one year for Christmas when it clicked in. What did the giraffe mean for me?

The giraffe is meant to teach us confidence, self love and self acceptance. It is here to show us how to walk with our heads held high. Being graceful and gentle unless provoked. Those that have the giraffe as one of their animals, know how to see the bigger picture of things. They are protective of their family and friends.

They ask you to have patience in all of the things that you do and to listen to your intuition more. Giraffe people can be sensitive but they are also empathic and understanding of others feelings and what they are going through, having a big heart that they wear on their sleeve.

For anyone who knows me they would know that this is me to a T. If I had only learned what this beautiful animal was trying to teach me when I was growing up I think my mindset would have been different. Maybe I would have gained the confidence in myself to make it a core belief at a young age instead of fighting hard to have it as an adult.

We took a family trip to the Denver Zoo during one of the breaks the kids had from school in 2018. There was some show going on with one of the other exhibits so we were enjoying watching the giraffe roam around his pen. A peacock entered into his pen and the giraffe did not like that. He ran around chasing him, trying to stomp him. They went around in circles until the peacock got out. It was one of the craziest things I have ever seen an animal do in real life and it was not something that I was expecting from a giraffe, I always thought of them as one of the most gentlest animals but then when I looked inside myself I can see the protectiveness of what is theirs.

I see the giraffe as my totem animal. A totem animal can be just one person or it can be referring to a group of people. An animal totem is used as symbol for the characteristics, and qualities that those people or person in that group share. I find this beneficial because if something has been weighing in on my mind, and then I see a giraffe. I know that I need to remind myself of those qualities.

Spirit Guides

Another animal that I have an association with on a spiritual level is the penguin. One day as I was doing a meditation I asked the Universe to please show me what animal represents my marriage. It was a cute penguin the ones that you see off of *Happy Feet*. Penguins bring with them the message to keep your eyes on your goals and dreams because they are worth it. If you look at where the penguin lives then you no doubt see that they can make it through even the toughest of conditions. They make great partners, very faithful, mating for life with only one other. They share the parenting responsibilities for the care of their young. Penguins know how to have fun with each other, and be affectionate. The penguin is one of my spiritual guides.

Animal Messengers

Our animal messages show up more than just meditations though. They also meet with us in our waking life. In the summertime when we put out the hummingbird feeders we are sure to get a few hummingbirds but some mornings when I walk out the door there is a hummingbird fluttering right in front of me as if he had been waiting to tell me something. For me he is telling me to be more loving, to give more love to those around me and to be flexible with the things that are going on. For some they are a sign of positive change or seeing the beauty in life. You will have to see what each one is meaning for you.

A fox is a good example of that. When my husband and I are riding together talking about how our day is going to go some mornings we are greeted by some sort of animal. Some mornings I see the fox, some he does and others we see together. This one is really interesting to me because when my husband see it is a message for him that today at work he needs to listen to his intuition and also blend in with his surroundings and just observe.

For me on the other hand it means I am in for a fun and playful day. I will come into contact with many people and am asked to bring play and laughter into their life.

The Cicada was probably the first spirit messenger that I found out that the Universe would do anything to get my attention when I asked for help.

Over the course of a few days I kept seeing animals that represented rebirth and transformation (not found in the snake but he made his message known to me too). I was sitting outside of my house on a warm summer morning. I was just enjoying a few minutes before I was going to wake the kids up for our outing to the park. I was thinking that instead of volunteering the next school year that I was going to be a substitute teacher. I had a lot of paperwork that I was going to need to gather and in truth I was scared because I had never subbed before. It was right then that out of the sky a Cicada dropped down DEAD on my bare thigh! I freaked!!! I was screaming and jumping up flinging the thing off of me. I swear I must have looked like a little chicken running around in circles, arms flying through the air yelling about the sky that is falling, the sky is falling! After a few moments I regained my composure and decided to see what it was (at the time I just knew it was a big bug) I have grey gravel so it blended in a bit but I found it. I grabbed a stick and got on my knees and started poking it to see if it was alive. I realized it was a cicada at that time, I had seen them before just not that close and usually there were more but this guy was all by himself. He looked big and old. I sent a picture of him to my husband who was very surprised that it was there because in our area they aren't very common.

His message to me was to go forth even though there was fear, I was going through a transformation and changes and he gave his life telling me that they were the right ones. Even though I felt lost, enlightenment was just around the corner. He was right.

I have a sketchbook and sometimes in the mornings I will sit and see what animal comes to me, or if I am driving the car sometimes I will be thinking about something and then there will be a car that comes by and it has an animal on it. The kangaroo is one that I see on the side of trucks when I am trying to plan my future goals. His message to me is about manifestation, taking leaps of faith and having nothing to worry about because it will happen.

These are all my daily helpers, my communication with the Universe when it is trying to get my attention.

Power Animals

When we came here, we were gifted so many guides, helpers, ancestors and angels to help us along our path. A power animal is very similar to an angel. There job is to help protect you from harm, illness and negative energy. But it also is here to offer you it's wisdom and characteristics to help you any situation. They can aid you in calling upon these inner strengths to move you forward in life. My power animal is the white Siberian tiger. When she appears I know for me that the message is I can overcome any obstacles and challenges that I might be facing. It is reminding me to use my personal power, and daring me to be brave. For others that share the tiger it might be reminding you not to be to aggressive with others or a warning that a possible threat is going on and it is asking you to have the courage to face it.

I would recommend in one of your tiny notebooks writing down some of the animals that you encounter as you go about your day along with the angel numbers, then at the end of the day or during your free time look up what each one means. Don't just go with the first website you find. Try a few and see which ones resonate with you, write down what their messages are and see if they have similar meanings or if you have different messages. Make sure that you put the date at the top because sometimes what they are telling us about is not meant until a few weeks or even months from now.

Whenever you are going through anything you always have the ability to call upon any of the animals to shift your energy into the qualities that you are needing at that time. For example if you are going to be doing any kind of public speaking then you can call upon the flamingo to be filled with his qualities. Which would be shining on the stage, showing your beautiful colors and bringing out your best qualities.

There are many ways that you can use the power of animals to help guide you through your human journey.

If you have trouble finding where to start, go buy a book on Native American astrology. It was there that I started. Mine is the hawk which a part of me knew already. Now we have a few that live around my house but they only show up when I need them.

My husband's animal is in that same book which is a bear. Again we already knew that. I think a bear is also his power animal because it is very strong inside of him. He can be sweet and loving towards his honey (yes that is a pun, I am his honey) like Winnie the pooh, or if you wake him during his nap he can transform into a grizzly bear.

Songs

Another way that signs may show up for us is through songs. If you are thinking of something and listening to the radio it is not coincidence that a song came on that tugs at your heart. It was meant for you to hear it.

Maybe you don't hear the song on the radio, maybe for no reason at all a song starts playing in your head. That is also a way that a message may appear and it is just as valid as any of the other ones.

Sometimes you may be thinking about something and then that day or the next day you talk to someone who brings up a similar idea and you say *I was just thinking about that*, again you put it out there to the Universe and now it is answering you.

One of the things that I enjoy doing is going to the Salvation Army. When I get into the parking lot I will sit there for a moment and have a conversation with the Universe/ God and I will say *If there is anything that you want me to know, anything that you wish for me to learn or do please let me be guided to the book that will help me.* Then I go inside.

Most days I come out with one or two books and some days it is a bag full because they each had something to teach me. Movies are the same way you can ask to be guided to a movie that will help you on your journey and then you go to Netflix and pick the one that you are drawn to.

You might get a letter in the mail, or an email that just hits this part inside of you that *Ah Ha* when that happens, listen to it.

What is the next step that you can take now?

CHAPTER 14

Spirit Guides and Soul Guides

Let me first state this by giving you some definitions The first one that I want to share with you is the definition of God: *The supreme or ultimate reality*. Being perfect in power, wisdom and goodness who is worshiped as creator and ruler of the universe.

It was the <u>*Power of Now*</u> that taught me that people associate God with their own mental images. No matter which way you see him though it is still the same, he will show up how you need him.

The higher self according to Wikipedia: It is a term associated with multiple belief systems, but its basic premise describes an eternal, omnipotent, conscious, and intelligent being, who is one's real self. Blavatsky formally defined the higher self as "Atma (the essence) the inseparable ray of the Universe and one self. It is the God above, more than within us". Each and every individual has a higher self.

When I first learned anything about having guides I decided to do a meditation that will introduce me to my guide. It was this Indian woman, she was very pretty, kind and wise. Each time I did a meditation to meet with her and talk she was different, changing more and more. One of the things that you have to do is ask your guides if you have permission to talk about them. I had permission with my tiger whose name is Lola by the way. But she told me no. After a few times meeting with her I asked her name and she told me Nova. Something with that really hit home in me. The name Nova means a star showing a sudden large increase in brightness and then slowly returning to its original state over a few months. I didn't put much into it though because I just thought it was a beautiful name.

For months she kept changing, until one day I went to meet her and she turned and looked at me and it was me! I was confused.

Why do you look like me? I asked.

"Because I am you, I am your soul, your higher self." she said I said (how is that even supposed to go?)

I don't understand you weren't before.

"I have always been."

Then why didn't you tell me? I asked.

"You wouldn't have listened to your own advice, you would have questioned instead of taking action."

I remember how excited I was when I learned this. I went to go see some of my friends and share it with them. I needed someone to tell this *Ah ha* moment too. I could see the point on why my soul did that though. If I knew in the beginning that all of this amazing advice was coming from me I probably would have tossed it out and not moved forward.

The summitlighthouse.org says this:

Christhood – The individual expression of the universal Christ consciousness. On the spiritual path, the individual Christ self, the personal Christ, is the initiator of the soul. When the individual passes certain initiations on the path of Christhood, he or she earns the right to be called a Christed one and gains the title of Son or Daughter of God.

Christ Consciousness the consciousness or awareness of the self in and as the Christ, the attainment of a level of consciousness commensurate with that which was realized by Jesus, the Christ. The Christ consciousness is the realization within the soul of that mind which was in Jesus Christ.

Christ self – The Higher self; our inner teacher, guardian, friend and advocate before God; the Universal Christ which the soul must rise. The Christ Self is the mediator between the individual and God.

Spirit Guides – They help you out any time during your life for any length of time on your human journey. They help you become a better person. They may be here just when they are needed or they may stay with you your whole life. They are positive beings here to help you spread light and love for the highest good of all. You must understand that if it is not loving, kind or for the good of all then it is not them. They are meant to guide you, offering advice never telling you to harm yourself or others. They can come in any form. If you have a monk as one of yours then that is ok (yes, I do), if you have a British queen that is ok too (no I don't, but I do have a friend who does).

Ascended masters – They were enlightened beings on Earth who spiritually transformed. Their job that they have for us is to raise our vibration in order to bring about greater growth in ourselves, and guiding us towards enlightenment.

The Buddha is a perfect example of an ascended master. Even he told others not to follow him but to find their own way. The Archangels are considered enlightened beings, so is John the Baptist. Any of the saints can be as well. They will show up in whatever form you need, if you ask they will come. Just like in the movie *The field of dreams* "if you build it they will come."

Ancestors – they are connected through our genetic memories. They help with family patterns and family karma, and trauma and they are here to help aid in the repairs that you need. If you had a grandparent that you were very fond of and then you suddenly lost them, it can be very painful. The bond that you had while they were here doesn't have to leave just because their body did. You can connect with them and still receive their guidance.

Soul Guides

The next one that we are going to talk about is Soul guides. Now I am not sure if there is another meaning to this but this is what I first came up with when I met one of my soul guides. A soul guide can be anyone. They are someone who your soul knows, not your human self but your soul. When they talk about certain things you understand them at a level that is beyond your human mind. They can be one for you and you can be one for them at the same time or you may switch roles during different times.

We are all in this together. We all have our demons that we have to fight, our own pain and struggles. We are all here learning and growing together and by sharing what we have used as a tool to help us and the struggles that we have faced makes us heal faster and not feel alone in it. While we are never alone because we have so much Universal love and guidance it is nice to know that there are physical guides here to help us along too. They could be your family, friends, co-workers, your life coach, therapist, or even just someone on the street who you talk to for a few minutes on your way to getting your morning coffee.

Our Guides Advice:

I have asked others 3 questions, some are worded a little differently but they all lead to the answers and tools that our souls are asking about.

We will start off with the wonderful Bernadette Logue from The Daily Positive. She is a transformation coach, author and soul guide. She is an inspiration to all souls. I love how she makes everything make sense, her uplifting energy is so contagious, her aura is beautiful colors of truth and enlightenment and her words have the power to change lives.

1. What is the biggest challenge or lesson that you think you have had while on this Earth Journey?

B's response – Realizing that the limiting beliefs and fears I was living with were not higher truth and yet they were creating my reality. Realizing that I had immense inner power to change my mind, to free myself of these inner limitations and that my outer life experience would change as a result.

Plus seeing that all challenges and hard-learned lessons like this are actually powerful vehicles for our evolution. What most challenges us in life can be a portal for liberation and can be the path through which we can become more soul aligned.

2. Is there a tool that you have used such as a mantra, chant, prayer, meditation, quote or technique that has offered you immediate results while in the middle of a challenge?

B's response – There are two tools/resources that have had a profound influence on me, bringing me a great deal of peace during any type of challenge. They are my go-to resources:

1. Tapping (also known as EFT) – this is so powerful for processing and releasing difficult feelings like fear, stress anxiety.

2. A Course in Miracles – this has been so impactful in terms of spiritual and psychological development and freedom, helping me to live courageously from my soul.

3. What is some wisdom that you would like to share with all souls?

B's response – Anything limiting or negative that you believe about yourself is not higher truth, it's not the soul you are, it's not who you were born as. It's baggage and mind conditioning that gets accumulated along the way in life.

No matter what has happened to us on this life journey, what we got or did not get, what we have done or not done, we are all here to rise beyond the negative mind conditioning, to return to the divine truth of who we really are.

The next one that I asked is my very good friend who is a teacher. I admire her outlook on life and always learn something from her. She is amazing in so many ways and I am very lucky that she is my friend. She guards a secret with her life. She doesn't judge, accepts everyone, and is a loyal and protective friend. She has this massively big heart and is like a mother to all the kids that cross her path. There is not a single kid that I know that has had her and not had their changes in a positive way. She is tough when she needs to be, fun and adventurous. She is one who always encourages me, she celebrates in my joys as if they were her own. She is a dolphin person and if you know the personality, enlightenment, and gentle nature of the dolphin then you will know how incredible this woman is.

Her name I Ashley Rupp and here is what she says:

1. What has been your biggest soul lesson or soul challenge that you have had to face?

Ashley's response – Moderation has always been my soul lesson and challenge. I'm the type of person who will try to do everything at once. I'll start a project and then start another one, and soon I have 10 projects started before I round back around to the first project and finish it. In turn, it carries with my soul. I stretch myself in so many directions with work, social, emotional, and physical that it comes down to my body having to tell me to take a break and rest. When I had the soul reading done, and that was a life lesson I was to focus on, I thought to myself JEEZ, the universe is telling me what I already know I struggle with. I really need to find this balance my soul needs.

2. What tool has brought you immediate help with dealing with this challenge such as a mantra, prayer, chant, quote, energetic tool, mediation, or visualization?

Ashley's response – I would have to say my number one tool has been my dear friend and mentor, Sarah. Without her guidance and knowledge, I honestly know I would not be as in-tuned with myself. She introduces new ideas and techniques that she is learning and using in her own practice. Also, knowing that my soul is searching and learning to relax, I put that into perspective with everyday life. I find myself asking the world to help guide me in the right direction, I seek knowledge through everyday choices, and I especially seek understanding through my dreams. In turn, I've spread it to my students in my classroom. We have mindful Mondays and focus on good energy and meditation. I want them to understand loving yourself comes before loving others. Being the best you can be, so that others love who you are. Also, I feel like it helps center myself with them. A continuous practice of taking care of your mind, body and soul.

3. What piece of wisdom do you want to share with all souls who are here on this human/Earth journey?

Ashley – My first response, What wisdom do I HAVE to share!

We are all on this planet, and have been given this body. What we choose to do with it, is our choice. Live each day wondering "how can I make the most of it."

The next one comes from my mom. Her name is **Carol Rackay.** She had to deal with difficult challenges that I hope no mother has to face. I can't even imagine the pain and suffering that she went through not being able to have a relationship with some of the people that she cared so much about. She dealt with her sufferings very silently as she was processing and overcoming some of the painful emotions. As mothers we give of ourselves in so many ways. My mom is more selfless as a mother than I am. She will give that last piece of cake even if she wants it. She will give what money she has even if she needs it. She will help you even if she is busy. She will take the blame for something before she throws someone under the bus. She is where I learned to try to find the bright side of any situation and to never give up hope. She understands my insecurities and isn't judgmental about them. When she goes through difficult times she tries to keep to herself handling things in her own way and in her own time. She has strength inside of her that is beyond my comprehension. A woman who I admire for her silent service for the greater good of all.

1. What has been your biggest challenge or soul lesson that you have gone through?

Mom – Having to let go of people and things that make you physically ill.

(The stress in trying to deal with the painful situation was making her throw up)

2. What is a tool that you have used such as a chant, mantra, quote, affirmation, mediation, prayer, visualization or energetic tool that has brought you immediate relief during the challenge?

Mom – I would say more than likely chanting let it go to myself to get the relief I needed. (mantra) I also kept saying "She is just not worth it."

3. What is a piece of wisdom that you would like to share with all souls to help them on their Earth journey?

Mom – To find your internal peace and be happy. Try not to let others keep you down.

The next soul guide is the art teacher at an elementary school. Her name is Brandy Davis. She is one that when you are having a tough day, her spirit is so strong that her energy will lift up yours when you are around her for more than five minutes. Even when challenging things are going on around her, she is calm. She keeps her center even when the storms are strong. She smiles at everyone she sees, having a glow that can be seen for miles and the way she expresses herself through her art is amazing. I admire her confidence and creativity in all that she does; a giving and helpful soul. I have gone to her many times for advice, another good protector of secrets. I watched her protect the secrets of even those who have done her wrong, never trying to get revenge, and still offering help to them. Those are qualities that are seen in the rarest of humankind and are all characteristics that I hope all of us will one day have.

1. What has been your biggest soul lesson or challenge that you have had to deal with on this earth journey?

Brandy – My lesson is probably self-love. I spend more time making sure everyone else has what they need.

2. What is a tool that you have used such as a chant, mantra, quote, affirmation, mediation, prayer, visualization or energetic tool that has brought you immediate relief during the challenge?

Brandy – Visualization and meditation are big tools I use always. I guess art is just a natural tool that I don't even think of as a self-mediation because it's just something I do. So, yes, art is a huge tool too!

3. What is a piece of wisdom that you would like to share with all souls to help them on this Earth journey?

Brandy – Be like a river and move with flow.

The next soul guide that I have is my Reiki master and friend. Her name is **Fiona Thieking. She is the one I call Sensay**, not Sensei like a martial arts teacher. She teaches through her words and actions. Her words enlighten me when I hear them. They are very powerful whether she says them out loud, in a text or email, and I feel that they need to be heard by all of us to look at the world in a different light. She changes the world just by her presence in it. Pushing us to be who we are truly meant to be, and to learn from all the mistakes that we make. Using them as lessons and ways to grow, not ways to play small or the victim. She is fearless, going into pain and suffering as if she were untouchable and using it for her highest good as well as everyone else's.

1. What has been your biggest soul lesson or challenge that you have had to face, or what challenges do you see other souls struggling with?

Sensay – My biggest soul lesson has been around self worth; trusting my own truths, setting boundaries to honor my truths, & staying consistent with "feeding the good wolf" so that I am in my highest alignment as much as possible. I notice that this is often a common denominator for other people as well. Oftentimes we "know" what needs to be done to improve our lives, but we either doubt ourselves or lack the follow through to overcome temptations of playing back into the old/past self. Evolving into the higher self is a moment to moment process that takes dedication, & my experience is that we eb & flow in & out of old self & new self until one begins to overcome the battle.

2. What tool have you used that has helped bring you immediate relief during the challenge, such as: mantra, prayer, chant, quote, energetic tool, or mediation?

Sensay – My go to tool is always Reiki. I envision myself surrounded by white & healing light, as well as all of my guides & angels; & then I set the intention that I will learn my deepest lessons inside of this challenge. The biggest piece of this is 100% trusting that I am supported & loved,&, that all that happens here (in this difficult space) is inevitably designed to awaken my soul.

3. What piece of wisdom would you like to share with all souls that are here on this human/ Earth journey?

Sensay – If there is one piece of wisdom I wish the conscious collective would understand at this time, it is the importance of the Mind-Body-Spirit Trinity. The mind, the body, & the spirit all open us to different awarenesses, but when one is blocked it trickles into the others. A healthy mind is supported by a vital body & a vibrant spirit, a healthy body is supported by beautiful thoughts & dazzling soul energy,& a healthy spirit is supported by a balanced mind & body complex. We are multidimensional beings inside of a human experience,& when our sacred trinity is out of balance it becomes difficult to remember this truth. My hope is that through awareness of all parts of our being, we may awaken to our truest potential, which is multidimensional.

The next one is from the amazing Susann Shier Taylor. She is the author of _Soul Mastery: Accessing the Gifts of Your Soul_ which is an incredible book. Literally it enlightens you as you read through the pages. I emailed her asking her if she would be willing to answer a few questions for me. Not only did she talk on the phone with me but she taught me more about my soul, where it came from and went into the areas that I didn't have the courage to look into myself. When we talked she knew that when I read that book of hers, that I was confused because in each one there were things that sounded like me. I didn't share this information with her, but she knew. She explained it is because my soul is both a Parallel and Hadrian. By knowing this I learned even more about my soul.

She didn't answer the questions in the same order as some of the others. Instead she wanted to offer the wisdom first.

1. What is a piece of wisdom that you would like to share with all souls on this earth journey?

Susann's response – Each person came here from other dimensions, each person has soul gifts and strengths that they wish to bring and their soul challenge is that the only wound they have is the wound of separation from their soul and the Universe that ultimately feeds us.

Our destiny is filled when we feel guided by our heart and soul and I consider enlightenment to be, being in love with life itself.

2. What tool have you used that has helped bring you immediate relief during the challenge such as a chant, mantra, prayer, mediation, visualization, quote, affirmation or energetic tool?

Susann – One of the things that for 20 years I have been working in Soul Mastery that I do for people, that they have found immediate relief for many and permanent relief is taking people on a journey to their home world and taking them on a journey to receive the resources that they need in that moment. Be it confidence, support, love, peace, abundance. It's a guided meditation journey. (you can find this mediation on her website at soulmastery.net, it's an mp3). *Called Soul Radiance.*

Me – This can bring permanent relief?

Susann – Yes, because it brings the parts of us that are hurt, abandoned and fear are crying out for a resource that can allow them to know that they are held and honored. It gives them exactly what they are looking for from Spirit which is unconditional love and acceptance. You can never feel accepted by a human being, the only thing that is going to give us acceptance is through the Divine. There is no human being that can give you the acceptance to the degree that you need, it can only come from the Universe.

3. What has been your biggest soul lesson or soul challenge that you have had to face while on this Earth journey?

Susann – Let me give you some history on me. I know that my mother tried to abort me while I was in the womb during this lifetime. My dad said we had too many children. So I came into this world feeling unloved and unwanted. Theoretically, I discovered that that was a soul wound and really was not just something that my mother and father put upon me. When I went back to that soul level of the womb to realize that I came to the with that sense of feeling I won't be loved and wanted here and repaired it at that level. Then I could start to receive Divine love and know that I was wanted and loved by not just the Universe but many beings and then it all turned around and obviously I am loved and wanted by thousands of people. But it wasn't about my parents it was about my soul wound. I had to take responsibility that I created it, not them and then I just forgave myself for what I wasn't connected to. Then I just got reconnected to the divine as a way to resolve it. I had to keep reminding my subconscious at times that I am loved and wanted. That is key because these old patterns come up but reminding myself that I am loved and wanted isn't just an intellectual intention and a statement "oh no you are loved and wanted" but when you feel the embodied place of being loved and wanted by Divine love or the Universe and I feel that in myself, especially in my heart then you know it as real. It's not just an intellectual belief that I am trying to convince myself is true.

This one is from my sister in law. She has faced many obstacles in her life but has always managed to pull through them with some tears and laughter at the same time. She has come out on top where others faced with the same things have failed. Fiercely independent, strong on all levels and yet still a kind and giving soul. She has this wonderful ability of seeing things from all perspectives and isn't just my sis in law she is my friend (my Machicka don't ask, we are strange souls). She was a teenage mother with little to no help from the fathers, getting a job as soon as she found out she was pregnant (after morning sickness it was bad). Always holding a steady job, getting her

GED and not only going for her goals but achieving them against all odds.

Her name is Jessica Watkins.

1. What has been your biggest soul challenge or lesson?

Jess – Even though I am still working on it. Accepting my faults, failures and my past (my decisions and others that affected me) then forgiving myself. After which I have the ability to decide to change because only I can do this for myself. I get every day to do a little better so one day I can be the best person I can be with nothing holding me back or any more excuses. And part of that is to give the same gift of acceptance and forgiveness to others.

2. What is a tool that you have used that has helped you receive immediate help during the challenge such as a mantra, chant, prayer, mediation, quote, affirmation, or energetic tool?

Jess – Can I change it? Do I need to accept it? Or do I accept it so I can change it later? Life is too short to keep negative energy thoughts (you taught me that) and how does this affect me and who else does it affect?

3. What is a piece of soul wisdom that you wish to share with all souls on this Earth journey?

Jess – Your past doesn't have to define or stop you. It was challenges and lessons so you can work on the present and towards the future you want with the wisdom you gained then every day after that.

The next one comes from His Holiness the Dalai Lama. I have always been very interested in the Buddhist way of life. I am not familiar with their religion nor do I try to pretend that I am. I do however find the concepts that they live by very fascinating. I have listened to the Dalai Lama and have read many of his books. **It is so wonderful that he has agreed to say a few words for this book and I hope that he empowers you the way that he does me.**

1. What is the biggest soul challenge that you see with us humans?

His Holiness – The biggest soul challenge today is not being able to rest enough from the rat race in our fast paced life in the materialist consumerist lifestyle. We expect the results of our work almost instantly like an automated machine. We need to learn to slow down and give ourselves the time to gain our health and restore our calm and compassionate spirit.

2. Is there a tool that you have used to help in the challenge such as a mantra, chant, prayer, mediation, quote, affirmation or energetic tool that you have used to get immediate results?

His Holiness – There is no mantra or prayers to heal ourselves from the rat race, except to learn to breathe calmly and stay focused on our duty for the welfare of humanity. But yes, the mantra of Lady Green Tara, who personifies the energy and activity of all the Buddhas which may be helpful for accomplishing our desired goal while eliminating the obstacles to that goal: OM TARE TUT TARE TURE SVAHA.

It is also a good idea to recite it for those suffering from the dreaded coronavirus outbreak these days.

3. What is a piece of wisdom that you would like to share with all souls while on this human journey?

His Holiness – Be kind to others and it's always possible to do that. Compassion is the ultimate source of our happy and fulfilled life. If you want to be happy, practice compassion. If you want happiness for others, practice compassion. Whatever you wish to achieve in your life, be realistic and optimistic. To that end have a positive vision of your life to be of help to others; be determined to achieve that good aim in life. Never give up. You may follow this Tibetan adage "Fall nine times, rise up nine time!"

The last soul guide comes from my dad. He grew up in a tough situation, facing things that I couldn't imagine. My true belief with him though is that he had to so that way he could handle the horrors of this world that the rest of us have only seen in movies. He is what you would call a modern day hero, he doesn't have any traces of nuclear chemicals in his veins although I wouldn't be surprised. He has helped countless people in ways that he may never realize. His gifts and talents are far more than what normal humans have. With him you won't get the nurturing that you will from my mom. You get the other side, the push to move you forward. In this world I think you need both and he offers that missing piece. I admire and respect him. He has taught me so much, just in different ways. I stay in a place of positive thanks to my mom and a place of world understanding when stuff gets real thanks to him. He has taught me that it is all fine and well to be at peace with yourself, but also how to make some tough choices if that is what is needed. He has taught me to be strong and protective of my family, yet offer a warm hand of love to those who need it, even to strangers. He is the smartest man I know, having an IQ that could be matched to Einstein. If I have half the writing skills, book smarts and generosity that he does, I would be able to take over the world without a second thought. His bravery and courage that he uses to handle anything is a gift that all of us can learn but few have the guts to do it.

His name is Mark Rackay and this is what he has to say:

1. What has been your biggest soul challenge or soul lesson that you have had to learn while on this human journey?

Dad – The biggest challenge of my life (so far) relates to my growing up in a loveless place with a mother that did not want me. She punished me for my existence and blamed me for her unhappiness.

The first 8 years I was pushed off to Grandparents. This was a favorable place for me because these two people were the best anyone could ask for. Strong with wisdom, from being part of the greatest generation, and full of love for their grandson, they did the best they could for me.

After those first years, my mother and I were forced to live together. I should use the term "coexist" because we really did not share a life. The woman was angry with everyone and anything, never finding her own peace. She was physically abusive as well, always enjoying her "slap my face" time. My father was out of town on business most of the time. Whenever I went to him for help, she did not want to hear it. He felt I should be able to work it out with her.

I overcame her pressure on me by the time that I was 12. She had a slap fest on me, and I had reached the boiling over point. I struck her back, repeatedly. She never hit me again but she did tell my father, and his response was, "I told you he was getting too big for you to hit like that."

As I grew I became more and more distant. I never went to her for anything. I became very independent, avoiding home as much as a teenager could. By the time I was an adult, my contact with her was almost nonexistent. Her and I maintained no contact unless forced by a third party.

In 1994, my father died. My mother moved away with a boyfriend and I have had no contact with her since. The challenge for me was realizing that it was not my fault. I spent much of my youth trying to please her, and always falling short. If I did anything, it was always wrong or not enough. When I was sick, it was my fault. Everything bad in life was my fault. Basically, I ruined her life. I was angry that my father knew what went on, and did nothing to stop it or get rid of her. I had no person to turn to for help. I learned that I better be strong, and look to myself for answers. I actually thank her for having me grow up to be the strong and independent person that I am.

2. What tool have you used to bring you immediate help during the challenge such as a mantra, prayer, chant, mediation, visualization, affirmation, quote or energetic tool?

Dad – I worked in a very high stress industry for over 25 years. During that time I owned several businesses, had family obligations, and tried to maintain a home/family life. Bringing home a bad day and work problems leads to an unhappy home time.

A normal person sleeps 8 hours a day and spends 10 hours at work and the associated drive time. That leaves precious few hours in the day to spend on yourself and quality time at home. Do you really want to spend that time worrying about work?

What project awaits you tomorrow morning at the office? Where is your down time if you really never left?

My solution was right there at my desk in the office. Every night, right before I got up to leave the office, I would open the bottom drawer of my desk. Mentally, I would place all my unfinished work, files, problems, and worries associated with the job into the drawer. When everything was in the drawer, I closed the drawer and left for home.

Once home, never think of the things in that drawer, they cease to exist. Screen your calls at home, avoid calls from work. It is your time, and the boss does not pay you for home time.

The next morning upon arrival at work, open the drawer and let those problems out.

Do your best during the day to get as much work done as you can. If you take a man's money, you owe him a full and good day's work. Once again, lock up those problems in the drawer when you head home.

Some people like to talk about their day with their spouse when they get home. I have never shared my day with my wife. Our time together is too precious to spend reliving the events of a stressful day. I relate the telling of a stressful day's activity to having a person run up to you and punch you in the nose. Every time that you tell the story, it is like getting punched in the nose again. How many times do you want to get punched in the nose?

3. What is a piece of wisdom that you would like to share with all souls while here on this Earth journey?

Dad – My advice to others is to be strong. DO NOT share your problems with friends or family. Keep the problems to yourself.

You are the only person in charge of your destiny. It is you. No other person has the same destiny or life path as you. Why would you seek the advice of someone else, especially knowing they are on their own life path?

I feel people who look to others for answers are really looking for someone to blame when it goes south. If you can make bad decisions, and blame someone else for them because nothing is your fault .... You see where I am going with this. Look inside yourself to solve your own problems. Make a decision and do it. Follow through.

Even if you make a mistake, you will learn from it. Take the lesson you learned from the mistake and formulate a new answer. Remember that the people who you seek advice from are busy on their own little path of life, full of their own problems. While they may listen to yours and be sympathetic, they really don't care about your problems, nor do you really care about theirs. Admit that reality to yourself, accept it and take control of your own destiny.

Among the many things that my dad does he is also a very talented writer. I wanted to share one of the articles that he wrote for the newspaper.

The Science of Luck

Seems we have that one "lucky" person in our group. You know the one: always wins 50/50 raffle, catches the most and largest fish, harvests the biggest bull, yells "bingo" after only 5 numbers called. One thing for certain in my little group; it sure isn't me.

I have spent a lifetime in careers that are considered "uninsurable." Add to that my ever present, and very close personal relationship, with none other than Murphy, of Murphy's Law fame. Murph, as I call him through long association, has made sure that good luck shall never enter the equation whenever I am involved.

And yet, there are those folks who seem to own the golden egg laying goose. These folks will venture off into the great outdoors, ignorant to all the ever-present dangers, and never get so much a brush with adversity an adversity.

Believe it or not, there is apparently some science to luck. In recent years, researchers have conducted studies about why some people are lucky, and if it is possible to make yourself luckier. Some of these researchers have slaved over the "iron maiden" as Ruark used to call the typewriter, and share these insights with us.

Professor Richard Wiseman, of the University of Hertford-shire, and best selling author of the book Luck Facto, conducted a study of luck with over 1,00 participants.

Prof. Wiseman concluded that people could actually change their luck. Luck is not something paranormal in nature. It is something that we are creating by our thoughts and behavior. To prove the results of his study were accurate, Wiseman created what he dubbed "Luck School."

In Luck School, he taught unlucky people how to act more like lucky people do. The results were impressive. In total, 80 percent of the people who attended said their luck had increased. On average, those people estimated their luck had increased by 40 percent. Not only were the participants luckier, but they reported being happier as well. I can understand that one. There is nothing like a run of good luck to improve mood.

In his book, Luck Factor, Wiseman noted that lucky people act upon opportunities and take more chances in their lives. He found that unlucky people suffered from paralysis by analysis.

I found that theory could relate very well to survival situations. People, who are paralyzed by fear or indecision, have a tendency to do nothing. That equates to sitting around and waiting for the end to come, and doing nothing to save you from the situation. Perhaps this relates to the old optimist versus pessimist dilemma.

Your faithfully has always been, and probably always will be, a pessimist. No, I did not mail in my Publisher's Clearing House sweepstakes card, and I did not buy a lottery ticket. But, if you wish to improve your luck, optimism is the key.

In any life-threatening situation, the rules of 3 come into play. The first rule is nobody can survive more than 3 seconds without hope. When the grim reaper is at the door, and the bell is tolling, "giving up as many do, rather than deciding to fight, is where that 3 seconds comes into play. There is no luck involved, it is a fight or die survival mindset.

Being an eternal pessimist, I probably see the world more accurately than someone who is an optimist. However, optimistic people will see more opportunities that the pessimist has already dismissed. This is a perfect reason one must remain positive in a survival situation.

We must learn to listen to our gut. You know, those nagging hunches about "that's a bad person" or "we will never be able to climb that without falling." Almost 90 percent of the people studied said that they trusted their intuition when it came to relationships, 80 percent in career choices, and at least 20 percent when it came to financial choices.

When intuition comes most heavily into play, is when you have expertise in an area, such as outdoor survival. The brain may detect a pattern you have not consciously seen before, and you get a gut feeling. The wise opportunist will stop and listen to those gut feelings.

Those nagging gut feelings are best described in a book by Gavin DE Becker called The Gift Of Fear. I consider this book essential reading for any members of Law Enforcement or First Responders. Any person who is involved in the outdoor world would benefit from the knowledge contained in the pages of that book.

De Becker teaches us that our life is driven by fear, as it has shaped our mind and personality thus determining how we will react to an emergency situation. Learning how to "listen" to your gut is the basis to survive any desperate situation you may find yourself in.

We have all heard about, or owned one of, those special dogs that just love everyone. Everyone except that one guy. That one guy makes the dogs go crazy; growling, cowering, and trying to stay away from this person.

Later you find out, this guy robbed a couple liquor stores at gunpoint, and fled the territory. Everyone is quick to say how great the dog's perception was of that rotten person. That could not be further from the truth.

That beloved dog has no ability to detect a character claw in someone it just met, nor be able to sense evil. What that dog can sense is fear. It sensed the fear of the one person the dog knows better than anyone else in the whole world; you. Your gut was sending out that "fear signal" and your dog sensed it.

De Becker teaches us how to detect and listen to those gut instincts. Once you have learned how to capitalize on what your gut is telling you, you will learn how to act in accordance. This is one of the best survival skills you can learn on the way.

Never give into fear or panic. Examine the opportunities with an optimistic attitude, and carry forth, and you will probably find an increase in your "luck" in any outdoor survival situation.

Remember that if you encounter the erudite Mr. Murphy, that he brings only bad luck and misfortune with him. We all know that Murp does not really exist, and yet he is always there. I know he is always with me when I am outdoors. If one of you would like to take him for a while, I could use a break."

– Mark Rackay –

This last one is from me. I wasn't sure if I was going to add in mine but I thought it was best to share some of my struggles. That way you know that I have been there too and still go there at times it's part of being human.

1. What has been your biggest soul lesson or challenge?

Me – I have 3 that are all intertwined and affect every area of my life when I allow them to and they are insecurity, self love, and self acceptance.

I have always underestimated myself in all ways, playing too much of the victim and allowing myself to play small. I gave up, backed out and hide away in most areas of my life out of fear of being shamed for the things that I have done. While I am peaceful and loving now a large part of my life I wasn't. Being lost and afraid I said and did things that were horrible. I battled both depression and postpartum depression and felt like I wasn't good enough and didn't even deserve to buy myself make up even though I enjoyed wearing makeup. I was so hard on everyone and even more on myself.

2. What has been a tool that you have used that has brought immediate relief during the challenge?

Me – I would have to say breath work. When I remember to breathe I always calm down and am able to focus better on finding solutions to anything. Breathing is what pushes us through pain, fear, even child birth. It's free and a part of me. When I speak, if I stop and take that breath I don't say things that I will regret, I don't snap at the ones that I love and I don't allow myself to be mean to me either.

3. What is a piece of soul wisdom that you wish to share with all souls on this Earth journey?

Me – There are so many things. Laughter is the best medicine in any situation, forgiving yourself and others is the fastest way to inner peace. Becoming your own best friend with the words that you say to yourself is the difference between success and failure. Be your own friend, You are beautiful don't wait for someone else to tell you that. Try whatever you do just try. I know people say don't try, do but for me it's different. If I am at least trying then I am not giving up, giving up is failure. Yes, you will get hurt but do it anyway.

CHAPTER 15

Finding Your Soul Family

Just like the seasons spring, summer, fall and winter have themes and people that will be our family throughout our life. It was during the coronavirus world pandemic that I added this final chapter, with kids running around, work needing to be done, homeschooling and trying not to panic buy that I had some time to sit and think. I hope my editor and my friend Ashley doesn't let me repeat myself here with any of the information but if I do, take it as lessons that I was obviously still learning and see if they are similar to anything that you went through during that time or ever on your journey.

As I had all this homebound time since the whole world was shutting down I tried to discover the theme in it all. Was this another great depression? Was it a lesson on learning to budget and be self sufficient? Had I not been grateful about my life or was I neglecting people in my life? What imbalance was going on that led up to these events, because if I find out why it is happening, then it will all be over and I can just go back to my normal life. It wasn't a pattern because it was happening to the whole world, it had to be a theme. Where do you go when you need to figure out why something is happening now, you go back in history. You know you can't change it, nor should you try to but if you go into history then you have the opportunity to learn something, to let go of something, and most importantly you have the ability to stop history from repeating itself. know that some people are loners but they aren't meant to be. No one wants to be alone and all of us have this need inside to be connected with other people. Some people may also call this their *"tribe"* which in essence is just another way to say soul family. The members of our soul family may be our friends, co-workers, or even the people we encounter in the community. It could be someone we sit next to in church on Sundays or on the bus ride home. It is up to us to deepen those connections and allow them to be part of our lives.

Soul family members can give great advice but they tend to teach us without even realizing it. We observe them, admire them and aspire to have some of the qualities that they have. They inspire us, uplift us and can make us feel like we can touch the moon by a simple stretch of our hands. Picking out of the sky, like we would pick an apple off of a tree.

By understanding everything that we have learned so far with universal laws we know that the people who are a part of our lives are put there by a Divine source not by a freak accident. Even if you don't get along with all of the members of your "soul family" doesn't matter. They are all there to help you play out the next chapter in your story. You get to be the one who gives them the roles, but you needed them in order to accomplish certain soul missions.

These themes you will take with you for the rest of your life, they were more training as your soul learned and grew. Each of your stories all have different endings but there are certain experiences and challenges that you needed each other for.

Go back in time for a moment here with me. When you were a child who did you spend most of your time with, outside of your blood family?

I was blessed to live in a neighborhood where we all knew each other, and all of us were friends. We had block parties, bbq's and just outside playtime together. Everyone looked out for each other. I had a few different soul families on my block.

What is amazing is when you get families like this you get core lessons but also individual ones from each member of the family. The themes that they teach you are the lessons that shape you for the rest of your life.

The first one is the Calderon's, a wonderful family with good values, discipline, and success. I would have to say that one of the main themes that I learned from them is *Connection*.

They are Dominican so along with being able to cook up some amazing food, they speak Spanish. I still do not although I try. I went with them to Spanish Mass at the Church, to parties and family gatherings. Some could not speak more than a few words of English at first and I only spoke a few words of Spanish. I loved the music but couldn't understand the words. Never once did I feel out of place though. I was a welcomed member of the family. I was greeted with kisses on the cheek, handed a plate of food, I was taught the dance moves and someone always interpreted for me what was being said. I was expected to clean up after myself, and push in my chair like everyone else. I loved every moment of it. Each one also taught me a lesson.

Whitney: taught me about making wise choices, about standing up for what is right and doing the right thing even if it means standing alone and having confidence in myself and what a true friend really is. She was my first true friend. She is so kind, and gentle with her words even at a very young age. She is so funny, always making me laugh when I was sad or angry and she had a way of making me own my mistakes. I learned how to take responsibility for my actions. When I would act up in school or disobey my parents. She would call me out, pushing me to be my best self while still loving me as her friend. She taught me about independence. I loved seeing her on stage whether it was for a band concert or for the drama club in the summertime. She was a natural star and belonged on that stage.

Joyse: Taught me about fun, comfort and being myself. Joyse was never afraid to say what was on her mind and she made you laugh while she did it. She was always a great storyteller and she knew how to draw you in. She was that way just by being herself, she would push me to be myself too. You went to Whitney for some wise advice but Joyse is who you went to for comfort first then you heard what was on her mind too, and usually I had the best of both worlds. I got both of these amazing sisters at once and was able to get through anything.

Gladys (Mom) would be next here. I have so many little and big lessons from her. She was a bus driver and wonderful mother. She protected me as if I was one of her own and expected me to behave the same way as her own daughters. She made me fix my mistakes, but she was also there for me to. When I was in elementary school I had this bus driver who was being mean to me and I didn't understand why. This same bus driver happened to be a relative of the Calderon family so I felt like I shouldn't say anything. I said something to Whitney and she told mom. Mom went and talked to my bus driver without saying anything to me. From then on the bus driver was nice to me and we talked more. It was nice. I finally found out mom had something to do with it when she asked me how everything was going on the bus. She taught me to give respect and accept nothing less from anyone else. She taught me about respecting myself. I also learned perseverance from her. When she came here she had to work to be a citizen, she had to work to learn English. She was tough and didn't expect others to do things that she wasn't willing to do. She did get her green card, she does speak English and just like the rest of the family she is a hard worker.

Jose (dad): Such a hard working and fun man. I loved whenever he came home how he greeted me was singing Sarah Lee. No my middle name is not Lee but that is just what he called me and it always brought a smile to my face. Him and mom were the perfect parenting team. They were both fun and funny but you respected them and you obeyed them. He started a trucking company and had the most beautiful houses built for his family. Mom always kept them spotless as did the daughters. The whole family unit was perfect and he was the leader not only of the family that lived in the house but the extended family too. When he told you no, you knew better than to argue with him. He wasn't even one to raise his voice but you had a mad respect for him. I learned from him the importance of family, of talking with your family not just living in the same house as them. He also knew that I was struggling with reading and shared with me that he too had been a weak reader and that by reading out loud it will make me stronger. Thanks for that too!

The Williams family is another soul family of mine that are just a huge group of great souls. They all don't have the same last names anymore but they all have the same the theme that they share. When I think of them I think *"ohana"* which I got from Lilo and Stitch and means family and family means no one gets left behind or forgotten. Once you become a part of this family you are there for life. Whether you are living in the same state or on the other side of the world.

They would have disagreements and arguments but nothing ever stopped this family from getting together. They always let stuff go and move forward. The theme that I also learned from them was communication. They know how to express themselves, talking out things and if needed, making their opinions heard. That takes courage and I respect that. All of them are hard workers, and more fun to be around than any party that I have ever been to. Any gathering is full of laughter and sometimes karaoke. I don't remember anyone complaining or bad mouthing anyone else in the family. They play, joke and prank of course but family time is important to them and isn't wasted on trivial problems instead life is celebrated. They are goal getters, each one chasing and living the goals that they turned into reality.

Shelsey is one of the most kind and gentle souls that is here on Earth. She welcomes all into her home and her heart. I gave her the nickname Shelter for this reason. She is gentle with her words and doesn't even swear (I think I heard one once). She hums all the time. I love that about her it shows just how happy she is. I remember being at her house when she would be getting ready to go out and she would turn the stereo up with songs that made her jam out as she would be doing her makeup. She helped me with my fear of driving and even helped teach me with her beautiful Tiburon. You can't be around her and be uncomfortable or feel insecure she doesn't let you. She will be the one who makes your insecurities feel ok not judging you, but empowering you. I have IBS and in the Florida heat I had to go number 2 alot! I wasn't a fan of going anywhere other than at my house. Shelsey made me go to the bathroom at her house and laughed and joked with me until I did, she knew how bad my stomach aches would get and how afterwards I would feel better. All the William's' daughters are creative and talented, each have their own area of expertise. I think that they get it from their mom. Shelsey has really good fashion. She always had the right outfits for any occasion and everything would work together perfectly from the shoes to the earrings. I am grateful that she passed some of this along to me. Showing me how to express myself by the outfits that I piece together and have fun while doing so. I have learned from her about knowing when to be silent and when to speak my mind and not just letting anger be the one in control but doing things in a respectful way. She is now married to a wonderful man. She is hard at work in the business aspect of healthcare I believe, as a side job she handcrafts these beautiful scarves that I am lucky enough to have one.

Kar is the next one. She is the shortest of them all and prob-ably the wisest. Her talents are in all that she does and is the most skilled nail technician (seriously her gel nails are so beautiful Hollywood needs to get a hold of this girl). I love reading what she posts on Facebook, always sharing her wisdom and of course throwing in some laughter with each one. They all lost their mom a while back, Kar will post reminding us to stop and give mom a call because one day we will miss it. She inspired me to start a savings account for each one of my kids because thinking about their future is so important. I like the positive quotes she posts and the little bits of soul wisdom that she adds to it. Kar is a leader and stands out with the generosity that she shares with others, always trying to do her part not just with her own family but with the world as whole. She also taught me not to take everything so seriously, that some things in life you brush off and some you laugh off.

Angie is the oldest of the three sisters. She is also the toughest. I have always had an equal amount of fear and respect for her. If their family was set up like a mafia Shelsey would be your logic, negotiator and possibly the getaway driver, Kar would be your planner, your lookout and the one to sneak up into the action. While Angie would be like "the godfather" the one who would find the best course of action by using her wit, quick thinking and street smarts. She is the one who sees that everything gets done. I remember when Angie was pregnant with her first child. She had a full time job, and was going to college, nothing slowed her down. I admire her dedication to her family and friends. Angie knows that she is the leader of the family, her little sisters look up to her and adore her. She is very protective of her family. She showed me that when you let someone into your heart even when you are frustrated with them, you still have their back. This was taught by her example not by anything that she said or did but simply by her everyday actions. Angie is now a college grad, married with another wonderful child and is very successful in her creative career choice of interior design.

Mike, their dad of course taught me by the lessons that he was teaching his daughters, and whether he meant to or not he also taught me. His lessons were always doing the right things in any situation, putting others above yourself (which all the girls put others first). Another lesson he tried to teach us was using the windows to cool down the house. Yes, you were right some of the times when you came home we hurried up and turned off the air conditioner. It was hot! He taught me a core lesson too, I was seventeen and living in Florida at the time. A few of my friends and I were sitting outside at their picnic table. We started talking about texts and emails. He said to me "Don't ever put something in an email or text that you wouldn't post on a billboard for everyone to see, every day as they drive to work."

I took this lesson with not only what I put into words but also in what words leave my mouth. I literally won't say anything about anyone that I wouldn't say to their face. If I am upset with someone, my job is to calmly express the story I am telling to myself to the person who the story is about, not telling stories to everyone else. I never got to thank him for thanking him for that lesson, so Mike Williams if you are reading this thank you.

Their mom Penny always had a smile on. She was creative and funny. Tiny just like her daughters, but knew how to stand her ground. I remember one night when we were all over and had just finished playing hide and go seek in the dark (black bear???). I was at the table with Penny and we were just talking. All of a sudden she looks over at one of her daughters who was cuddled up asleep on the sofa with her boyfriend at the time. A boy who the rest of the family didn't approve of. She pointed and said "look how happy she is, how can I forbid him to come over and make her stay away from him." I didn't care too much for the boy either but I didn't say anything because it wasn't my place. I knew why the others didn't, they were just trying to protect her and they were right but thanks to Penny I saw the other side of it. She had a point with it. It was then that I understood there are two sides to every coin.

I have had many more people who have been a part of my journey in different roles. Some of these souls were my sisters, brothers, cousins, grandparents, and parents. Not by bloodlines but through energy strands. Invisible cords that link us to people who we have any kind of relationships with. These cords don't know anything about blood being thicker than water. These connections are the members of your soul family.

Ask yourself these questions:

Who are some of the people in your soul family?

What are some themes that your soul families have taught you? Do you use those lessons now? Why or why not?

What are things that you have taught them?

How have they Inspired you? How have they challenged you?

Once you have an understanding of who your soul family members are and the different roles and lessons that those members are here to help us go through, you will realize that you're not alone on this journey. A comforting reminder that we are all in this together, they to help you and you to help them.

REFERENCES AND RESOURCES

Thedailypositive.com

Mindvalley.com

Wikipedia.com

Onemindoneenergy.com

Gaia.com

Numerologist.com

Cafeastrology.com

Brenebrown.com

soulmastery.net

Mindbodygreen.com

Deepakchopra.com

Recommended Readings:

Midnights With the Mystic: A Little Guide to Freedom and Bliss by Cheryl Simone and Sadhguru Jaggi Vasudev

The Secret by Rhonda Byrne

The Power of Now: A Guide to Spiritual Enlightenment by Eckhart Tolle

Pinch Me: How Following The Signals Changed My Life (Follow The Signals) by Bernadette Logue

Going Out On A Limb: How Signals Led Me Beyond My Limits & Into Truth (Follow The Signals Book 2) by Bernadette Logue

Breaking the Habit of being yourself by Joe Dispenza

The life you were born to live by Dan Millman

Unleash Your Life: 166 Truths to Unlock Your Inner Peace, Freedom & Success by Bernadette Logue

The Untethered Soul: The Journey Beyond Yourself by Michael A. Singer

The Divine Matrix: Bridging Time, Space, Miracles, and Belief by Gregg Braden

The Law of Attraction: The Basics of the Teachings of Abraham by Esther Hicks

Soul Mastery: Accessing the Gifts of Your Soul (The Soul Mastery Trilogy) by Susann Taylor Shier

The Seven Spiritual Laws of Success: A Practical Guide to the Fulfillment of Your Dreams by Deepak Chopra

The Seat of the Soul by Gary Zukav

Recommended Movies:

The Secret

The Host

Disney's Inside Out

Defending your life